Essential Histories

The Wars of Spanish American Independence 1809–29

Essential Histories

The Wars of Spanish
American Independence
1809–29

John Fletcher

First published in Great Britain in 2013 by Osprey Publishing,
PO Box 883, Oxford, OX1 9PL, UK
PO Box 3985, New York, NY 10185-3985, USA
E-mail: info@ospreypublishing.com

Osprey Publishing is part of the Osprey Group

A CIP catalog record for this book is available from the
British Library

Print ISBN: 978 1 78200 766 1

PDF ebook ISBN: 978 1 78200 767 8
ePub ebook ISBN: 978 1 78200 768 5

Index by Zoe Ross
Typeset in ITC Stone Serif and Gill Sans
Maps by Peter Bull Art Studio
Originated by PDQ Media, Bungay, UK
Printed in China through Asia Pacific Offset Limited

13 14 15 16 17   10 9 8 7 6 5 4 3 2 1

Osprey Publishing is supporting the Woodland Trust, the UK's
leading woodland conservation charity, by funding the dedication
of trees.

Contents

Introduction

The Wars of Spanish American Independence were a series of simultaneous conflicts in Spain's North and South American colonies between 1809 and 1829. Started by the same set of causes, they were fought almost entirely independently within each of the four viceroyalties that comprised Spanish America. Those who fought for independence were called Patriots, while those who fought for the continuation of Spanish rule were called Royalists. Ultimately, Patriots prevailed in each viceroyalty and at the end of the wars the only colonies remaining in Spanish possession were Cuba and Puerto Rico. The conflicts marked the end of Spain's position as a world power and brought the nations of Mexico, Panama, Venezuela, Colombia, Ecuador, Peru, Bolivia, Chile, and Argentina into existence. Britain, the United States of America, and France benefited from the decline of Spanish influence through increased trade, influence and, in the case of the United States, territory.

The Royalist cause was complicated by the struggle within Spain between Conservative Absolutists and Liberal Constitutionalists.

Batalla de Maipú (detail), 1904, by Pedro Subercaseaux (1880–1956). The wars of independence, which divided Americans by caste, region, and political philosophy, were as much civil wars as rebellions against Spain. (Museo Histórico Nacional, Chile; photograph by Marco Benavente)

Constitutionalists believed corruption in the royal family was the cause of Spain's decline and sought to install a constitutional monarchy, while Absolutists strove to restore the old monarchy without change. During the wars each faction held power twice, leading to confusion and conflict among Royalist officials in the colonies. Royalist ranks were further strained by tensions between newly arriving officers from Spain and veteran officers in America. American officers found their new Spanish counterparts to be arrogant and ignorant of America and its people. Spanish officers recently arriving from the Napoleonic Wars were shocked by the amateur training of the American commanders and the bloodthirsty way in which they prosecuted the war. The resulting rivalries were fatal to the Royalist cause in Mexico, Venezuela, and Peru.

The Patriot cause was divided over the territorial boundaries of the new countries and constitutional issues regarding the strength of central government within each of the new nations. The definition of borders reflected the inevitable regional differences that arose with colonization of such an immense geographical area and the fact that huge portions of the Spanish colonies were barely explored, let alone settled, frontiers. The question of central government split Patriots into Federalists, those who wished to see weak central governments presiding over loose confederations of strong individual states, and Centralists, who believed in a strong federal government and limited states' rights. It took less than two years for the Patriots in New Granada to fall into civil war over this very issue and in 1815 a Federal League formed in opposition to the centralist policies of Río de la Plata. Besides weakening Patriot efforts, these divisions led to decades of instability and warfare after independence.

The wars were initiated and driven by members of the upper strata of colonial society: Peninsulares, whites born in Spain, and Creoles, whites born in the colonies. The majority of Peninsulares were Royalists while a smaller majority of Creoles were Patriots. Being at the top of the economic and social pyramid, these groups' divisions reflected who stood to gain or lose the most from the war's outcome. Among the lower castes, the situation was highly dependent on the region and the year. Both sides made appeals to draw the lower castes to their own banner. Royalists used laws ending Indian tribute, religion, and the semi-mythical status of the king to attract followers, while Patriots proposed legal equality and emancipation of slaves in exchange for service. In many cases loyalty was simply given to existing local leaders.

Despite the participation of over 40,000 Spanish regulars and 6,000 British and Irish mercenaries, the overwhelming majority of men who fought these wars were Americans. On the Patriot side two generals, Simón Bolívar and José de San Martín, emerged as the greatest military leaders, steadfastly remaining committed to their vision through every trial. Eventually, each became known as "The Liberator." The contributions of black and Indian soldiers deeply challenged the racial presumptions and caste structure of colonial society, and advanced the end of slavery in the Americas.

The wars divided into four phases. Phase 1 was the initial push for independence, 1810–13. This phase was marked by the declaration of independence of most Patriot regions and the first campaigns to drive out the Spanish. Phase 2 was the Royalist reconquest, 1814–17. This phase was marked by the arrival of Spanish troops in the region and the successful efforts of the various viceroys in reasserting the authority of the Crown across almost the entire region. Phase 3 was the Patriot triumph, 1818–24. This phase was marked by a snowballing series of political events and Patriot victories that secured independence. Phase 4 was consolidation, 1825–29. This phase was marked by the defeat of the final Royalist outposts and emerging conflict within and between the newly independent states, in many cases directly linked to the legacy of colonialism.

Chronology

1807 **November** French troops invade Portugal

1808 **February 10** French troop build-up in Spain
March 18 Spanish King Charles IV abdicates in favor of his son, Ferdinand VII
May 2 Anti-French riots in Madrid, Spain
May 5 During negotiations arbitrated by French Emperor Napoleon Bonaparte, Charles IV rescinds abdication while Ferdinand VII abdicates in favor of Charles IV; Charles IV then re-abdicates in favor of Napoleon
May 6 Ferdinand VII imprisoned in Bayonne, France; Charles IV accepts a French pension and eventually settles in Rome, where he dies on January 20, 1819
July 25 Napoleon names his brother Joseph king of Spain; the colonies refuse to acknowledge French rule
September 25 Supreme Central and Governmental Junta of Spain and the Indies formed in Seville, Spain to resist France and autonomously rule in Ferdinand VII's name until his restoration

1809 **May 25** Junta formed in Chuquisaca, Upper Peru
July 16 Junta formed in La Paz, Upper Peru
August 10 Junta formed in Quito, New Granada
September–October Royalist troops defeat La Paz and Chuquisaca juntas
December 4 Royalist troops enter Quito

1810 **May 25** Junta established in Buenos Aires, Río de la Plata
May–July Juntas formed across New Granada
September 16 Miguel Hidalgo issues "Grito de Dolores" in Dolores, New Spain
September 18 National Junta formed in Chile
September 22 Quito declares another junta
October 11 Quito junta declares independence
October 30 Patriot victory at the battle of Monte de las Cruces, New Spain
November 7 Royalist victory at the battle of Aculco, New Spain

1811 **January 17** Royalist victory at the battle of Calderón Bridge, New Spain
March 9 Royalist victory at the battle of Tacuarí, Paraguay

Batalla de Tacuarí, c. 1856, by Carlos Pablo Ripamonti (1874–1968). According to legend a 12-year-old drummer boy guided an officer blinded by cannon fire to safety during the battle of Tacuarí. The boy himself was killed. Most likely fiction, the story nevertheless sums up the deep human toll taken by the wars. (Archivo General de la Nación, Argentina)

Batalla de Chacabuco, 1863, by José Tomás Vandorsse. This painting depicts the climactic Patriot charge. In the foreground the 7th and 8th infantry regiments move forward, while the horse grenadiers attack in the background. Notice the segregated Patriot units and the infantry in garrison caps while the horse grenadiers wear shakos. (Museo Histórico Nacional, Chile)

June 20 Royalist victory at the battle of Huaqui, Upper Peru
July 5 Venezuela declares independence
July 30 Hidalgo is executed in Chihuahua, New Spain
November 11 Independence declared in Cartagena, New Granada

1812   **March 19** Cádiz Constitution, Spain
July 25 First Venezuelan Republic capitulates

1813   **February–August** "Admirable Campaign," Venezuela
March 15 Bolívar declares "War to the Death," Venezuela
August 7 Bolívar declares Second Venezuelan Republic
November 14 Royalist victory at the battle of Ayohuma, Upper Peru
December 5 Patriot victory at the battle of Araure, Venezuela

1814   **February 3** Royalist victory at the first battle of La Puerta, Venezuela
February 28 Patriot victory at the

first battle of San Mateo
March 22 Ferdinand VII restored to throne and Cádiz Constitution rescinded, Spain
March 25 Patriot victory at the second battle of San Mateo, Venezuela
May 14 Royalists capture Antonio Nariño in New Granada
May 28 Patriot victory at the first battle of Carabobo, Venezuela
June 15 Royalist victory at the second battle of La Puerta, Venezuela
June 23 Royalists surrender Montevideo, Banda Oriental
July 16 Royalists capture Caracas, Venezuela; fall of Second Venezuelan Republic
August 14 Pablo Morillo placed in charge of 10,000-man Spanish expedition
October 1–2 Royalist victory at the battle of Rancagua, Chile
December 5 Royalist victory at the battle of Urica, Venezuela

1815   **May 8** Bolívar exiled to Haiti
April 7 Pablo Morillo's "Expedicion Pacificadora" arrives in Venezuela
August–December Royalist victory at siege of Cartagena, New Grenada
November 28 Royalist victory at the battle of Viluma (Sipe Sipe), Upper Peru (Bolivia)

1816   **May** Morillo completes reconquest of New Granada
May 8 Bolívar voluntarily exiles himself to Jamaica, then Haiti
July 9 Independence declared by the United Provinces of the Río de la Plata
August 28 Portugese/Brazilian troops invade Banda Oriental

1817   **February 12** Patriot victory at the battle of Chacabuco, Chile
July 17 Patriots capture Angostura, Venezuela

1818   **March 16** Royalist victory at the third battle of La Puerta, Venezuela

April 5 Patriot victory at the battle of Maipú, Chile

1819 **August 7** Patriot victory at the battle of Boyacá, New Granada
December 17 Congress of Angostura declares creation of Gran Colombia

1820 **January 1** Riego Revolt, Spain
January 22 Portuguese victory at the battle of Tacuarembó, Banda Oriental
February 1 The battle of Cepeda marks the beginning of civil war in United Provinces of the Río de la Plata
March 10 Cádiz Constitution restored, Spain
November 26–27 Truce between Bolívar and Morillo; "War to the Death" rescinded
December 17 Morillo returns to Spain

1821 **June 24** Patriot victory at the second battle of Carabobo, Venezuela
September 27 Agustín de Iturbide enters Mexico City and declares Mexican independence

1822 **April 7** Patriot victory at the battle of Bombona, New Granada
May 24 Patriot victory at the battle of Pichincha, Quito
July 26–27 San Martín and Bolívar meet at the "Entrevista de Guayaquil"

1823 **July 24** Patriot victory at the battle of Lake Maracaibo
September 23 Ferdinand VII restored and Cádiz Constitution rescinded in Spain
December 2 USA proclaims Monroe Doctrine

1824 **December 9** Patriot victory at the battle of Ayacucho, Peru

1825 **April 1** Patriot victory at the battle of Tumulsa, Upper Peru
October 12 Uruguayan victory over Brazilian forces at the battle of Sarandí (in Brazil, previously part of Banda Oriental)

1826 **January 15** Royalist garrison surrenders, Chiloé, Chile
January 22 Royalist garrison surrenders, Callao, Peru

1829 **July 27–September 11** Mexican victory at the battle of Tampico, Mexico

Los Artilleros de Borgoño en la batalla de Maipú, 1943, by Pedro Subercaseaux (1880–1956). The expert handling of this Patriot artillery battery was crucial to stopping a Royalist counterattack and turning the tide of the battle. (Museo Histórico Nacional, Chile; photograph by Marco Benavente)

A creaking empire

In the predawn hours of August 1, 1806, a small fleet of ships disembarked about 600 armed American and British nationals, along with one Venezuelan, near Coro, Venezuela. The troops formed the vanguard of an army of liberation. The Venezuelan, Francisco de Miranda, was their commander. Miranda was an exiled Venezuelan Creole and tireless advocate for independence. He was 56 years old and a veteran of the Spanish and French armies, having begun his career as a captain and ending it a general. He had served in Africa, the American Revolutionary War, and the French Revolutionary Wars, and gained a reputation as a brave and capable officer. He was well known throughout the capitals of the world but, after 30 years abroad, was a virtual stranger to his own country.

Miranda had long ago deduced that Venezuela needed to be free of Spanish rule. He loathed the restrictions of Spanish government, the stifling of trade and ideas that kept Venezuela backwards and prevented the colony from developing to its full potential. During his years abroad he had received countless letters from wealthy Creoles that reinforced his view. Clearly the people of Venezuela – indeed, of all the Spanish colonies – would rise upon his arrival and claim their natural place in the Enlightenment-inspired realms of free trade and free nations.

To his dismay, he found Coro nearly deserted; not only had the garrison fled, so had most of the populace. After ten frustrating days of issuing bombastic decrees to a deserted town, Miranda realized his fundamental error: the complaints of his wealthy Creole contacts were not the grievances of the masses. As 1,500 Spanish troops gathered outside the town and additional reinforcements hurried forward from Caracas, Miranda sullenly re-embarked

Generalísimo Francisco de Miranda, 1899, by Emilio Jacinto Mauri (1885–1908). Miranda was a rising star in the French Revolutionary Wars until he fell foul of the Terror. His confident generalship in the Low Countries during 1792 and 1793 stands in contrast to his meek performance in Venezuela in 1812. (Palacio Federal Legislativo, Venezuela)

and beat an ignominious retreat back into exile. When the royal authorities reasserted control, they discovered a pile of manifestos Miranda had printed, including the banned "Declaration of the Rights of Man" – no one had bothered to distribute them, much less read them. Such was the fervor for independence in late 1806.

Miranda's experience was hardly unique. After three centuries of rule, Spanish officials had become adept at defusing colonial grievances by isolating groups and geographically containing disruptions or uprisings. This "divide and rule" strategy started with an exceedingly complex, racially based caste system. The inhabitants of the colonies were divided into groups, each of which was given its own sets of laws and restrictions, including the rights its members possessed, the occupations they could undertake, the institutions they could access, and even the education they could receive. At its most basic level, the caste system recognized four major racial groups – at the top were Peninsulares, whites born in Spain. Creoles, whites born in America, were second. The last two groups, Indians and blacks, were at the bottom. Racial intermingling was common and within a few generations the Spanish had created subcategories for every combination imaginable. The most common were Mestizos, children of a white and Indian union; Mulattos, offspring of white and black parents; and Zambos, those from black and Indian couplings. Eventually the terms Pardos ("half-breed") and Morenos ("dark-skinned") arose as shorthand to describe the various black and Mulatto combinations. Peninsulares held the highest posts and were favored in every instance. Creoles enjoyed considerable rank and privilege but were excluded from the highest rungs of power. Mestizos could aspire to most trades but suffered considerably restricted rights and status. Indians and blacks provided the menial labor that worked the mines, ranches, and plantations of the colonies.

Since the system was so obviously racist, mixed-race families would jealously guard any white heritage in order to remain in the highest available caste. Likewise, Creoles would downplay or disown any non-white ancestry to avoid slipping down the social ladder. Admittedly, within each caste it was possible for an exceptional individual to amass wealth or political power but the odds grew longer the further one was from white. Rare individuals could even petition the authorities – usually Peninsulares, sometimes Creoles, never one of their own – to grant them legally white racial status so as to allow their children to go to school or join a clerical order. For the vast majority, however, to be Indian or black was to be consigned to a life of hard labor and little comfort. Slavery was practiced throughout the colonies but emancipation was possible through any number of means, including

purchase by the slave himself. A freed slave was able to work as he or she saw fit within the limits of the caste system, and in regions where they composed a substantial proportion of the population, such as Cartagena in New Granada, free blacks enjoyed a considerable degree of wealth and power. While Indians were technically free, the vast majority were exploited through structural conditions such as the inability legally to quit a job or move off a parcel of land; these restrictions reduced them to bondage in all but name.

One institution whereby a man could escape the caste system was the military. After the Seven Years' War (1756–63), a series of colonial reforms were enacted to increase the efficiency of government, lower the costs of empire and strengthen the resiliency of the colonies if faced with unexpected crisis. One of these reforms was to replace standing garrisons of Spanish troops with local militias. The original intention was to form the militias from Peninsulares and Creoles, but it soon became apparent the system would have to be expanded to include non-whites. While the white inhabitants made up about 20 percent of the population, it was centered in the cities and the developed coastal regions. There were many places in the interior where there simply were not enough whites to form the required units, and segregated units of non-white troops quickly became commonplace. The authorities worried, however, about arming the very people the regime exploited for cheap labor and onerous tributes. The solution was found in the *fuero militar*, a separate judicial system granted by royal decree for members of the militia. This system was far more lenient, especially for officers, than the civil, caste-based, legal system. When applied to non-white militiamen, it offered a path to a better life than they could otherwise hope for. It was an effective, if accidental, model that proved its value across the colonies as non-white troops remained loyal to the Crown, helping to put down local uprisings rather than risk losing their newfound favored status.

Sistema de castas ("Caste System"), no date, artist unknown. This chart shows the various racial combinations used to peg status and rights in Spain's colonies. (Museo Nacional del Virreinato, Mexico; photograph by Alejandro Linares García)

The Catholic Church was another instrument used to maintain Spanish control. A series of papal bulls in the 15th and 16th centuries committed the Church to actively sermonizing on behalf of the Crown while ceding remarkable control to secular authorities by allowing royal authorities to appoint clergy in America. In exchange, the Church received the *fuero eclesiástico*, special legal rights and exemptions similar to the *fuero militar*. The Church became a core unifying force across all social strata and her decrees went a long way towards establishing the norms of society. In addition to the soft power of the pulpit, the Church wielded other, more tangible, assets that helped maintain the status quo. Among Creoles the Church was the primary lending institution, fulfilling the role of a bank with the same ability to grant or deny credit. The Church also imposed the Inquisition in the colonies to root out and suppress any literature or ideas that threatened the established order, especially material related to the Enlightenment or the French Revolution. Banned books were hunted down and burned and their possessors excommunicated, imprisoned, or referred to royal authority for punishment. For example, in 1793 the Inquisition caught a young Creole ideologue named Antonio Nariño (1765–1824) printing 100 copies of *The Declaration of the Rights of Man and of the Citizen*, a key document of the French Revolution. Nariño was convicted of treason and all copies of the work destroyed. While it could not entirely eliminate the flood of material arriving from Europe, the Inquisition severely limited its distribution and helped drive Creole agitators underground or overseas.

The Church assumed a more ambivalent role among the lower castes. There was a long tradition of parish priests protecting the Indians from the worst exploitations of the colonial system. Further, by the eve of independence many parish priests were from the lower castes themselves and had far more in common with their local congregation than the Church's upper hierarchy. On the

Plaza Mayor frente a la Catedral, 1845, by Augustin Challamel (1818–84). The physically imposing architecture reflected the dominance of Roman Catholicism and the Church in colonial society. Churches were omnipresent, from the smallest village to the greatest city. (Biblioteca Nacional del Perú)

El Himno Nacional ("The National Anthem"), no date, by Pedro Subercaseaux (1880–1956). Despite the structural limitations of the caste system, Creoles enjoyed a life of privilege and status comparable to that of the upper tiers of European society. (Museo Histórico Nacional, Argentina)

other hand, the Church had an equally long tradition of manipulating or repurposing theological material to encourage Indian docility and submission to the very system that exploited them. The case of the Virgin of Guadalupe stands out in particular. In the mid-17th century, the Church in New Spain began vigorously promoting allegedly miraculous appearances by the Virgin Mary to an Indian peasant just after the Spanish conquest. These appearances were packed with physical and metaphorical symbols promoting the transition of authority from the pre-conquest Aztec king and religion to the new Spanish king and Christian religion. In time, the symbolism of the story took on powerful nationalistic overtones for Mestizos and Creoles estranged from both the Spanish and Indian worlds. By the time of

Tipo blanco e indio mestizo, 1853, by Manuel María Paz (1820–1902). Daily routine led to an inevitable overlapping of caste and the consequent development of an American identity, distinct from Spain. (Biblioteca Nacional de Colombia)

independence, the Virgin of Guadalupe represented the very idea of what it meant to be Mexican. Other examples revolved around linking the veneration of saints and the role of Holy Days to previous indigenous traditions. In every case, there was a dual-track goal of expanding Christianity while legitimizing Spanish rule, fealty towards the Crown and Roman Catholic authority.

Despite these powerful institutional controls, tensions in the colonies during the latter half of the 18th century were deep and persistent. Many colonial complaints centered on economic issues. The list was long, sometimes affecting a single caste, sometimes all of them. Creole merchants chafed under the *comercio libre*, or free commerce, an ironically named set of economic-policy reforms that benefited Spain at the explicit expense of the colonies. Exports and trade were restricted to approved products and trading partners, while local industries were devastated by cheap imports. Meanwhile, Indians suffered forced tributes of both money and labor imposed by Corregidores, low-level colonial authorities, and Caciques, local Indian nobles retained within the Spanish system to keep control of the population as surrogate rulers.

Many local uprisings occurred with the aim of modifying or mitigating these economic burdens, the most powerful being one begun by Túpac Amaru in Peru in 1780. Túpac Amaru, a Jesuit-educated Cacique who was a descendant of the last Incan king, had become increasingly despondent over the tributes and forced labor exacted from his people. He kidnapped a local Corregidore and forced him to write to other local officials inviting them to a meeting near Cuzco, the ancient Inca city and colonial center of power. When 200 colonial functionaries showed up, Túpac Amaru had them all arrested, presented to a crowd, and executed. Túpac Amaru originally hoped to build a broad coalition of Indians, Mestizos, and Creoles united in

Guaduas, 1846, by Edward Walhouse Mark (1817–95). This illustration shows street vendors in the town of Guaduas, Colombia. Infrastructure was sparse and economic activity was tightly controlled to serve Spanish interests. Consequently, many areas were severely underdeveloped. (Banco de la República de Colombia)

shared injustice, but his Indian followers rampaged indiscriminately against any whites, and the terrified Creoles quickly fled for the protection of the viceroy. The Spanish responded to Túpac Amaru's initial victories by bringing in regular troops and Pardo militias from Lima and the other coastal regions. The brutal campaign that followed cost over 100,000 lives. Túpac Amaru was captured and executed in 1781, his dismembered body displayed in towns across the region, but the uprising was not finally quelled until 1783. It left Peruvian Creoles petrified of the lower castes, a fear that played a powerful role in determining Peru's strongly Royalist sentiment during independence.

Racial fears were driven home in New Spain and New Granada by the example of the Haitian Revolution of 1791. The initial slave uprising and subsequent war witnessed genocidal racial passions that eventually led to the near-eradication of all whites and the defeat of several European armies. Nervous slave owners all along the Caribbean coast cowered as they looked at their own farms and plantations, wary that any easing of

conditions would lead to similar results. Fear of racial violence, particularly black violence, was a constant worry throughout the wars of independence, shared by Creoles on both sides. This fear tempered the revolutions, causing Creoles to limit the practical benefits of independence to themselves, even as Indians and blacks increasingly filled the ranks fighting for that independence.

The examples of Túpac Amaru and Haiti were seen as reflections of the French Revolution – cautionary examples of extreme democracy leading to a frenzy of anarchy and ruin. The Creoles dreamed of a more controlled example, which many found in the American Revolution. Creoles saw the American Revolution as a more gentrified revolution enacted by a homogenous population acting in true Enlightenment fashion. Miranda summed up the sentiment in 1799: "We have before our eyes two great examples, the American and the French Revolutions. Let us prudently imitate the first and carefully shun the second" (Bethell 1985: III.46). The framework for all the colonies would be the same – independence for all, but true liberty and equality for Creoles only.

"Fight and you shall win"

Armies

Royalist and Patriot armies shared the same background. Both grew out of the Spanish system of colonial defense that had been implemented in the 1770s. That system called for a large number of local militia forces alongside a small number of Spanish regular army garrisons at key strategic locations, almost inevitably ports. When the wars began, the Royalists simply activated existing units. The Patriots usually created new units, but these were often based on old colonial organizations.

On paper, units were organized as their regular army counterparts in Spain, but local variations were common. Infantry were organized into regiments with one to three battalions. Each battalion had nine companies, with 80 men per company. Cavalry were organized into regiments containing four squadrons with three companies of 40 men each. Regiments were administrative units, while battalions and squadrons were the basic units of battle. Artillery was organized into companies

of about 100 men operating four cannon. It was common for artillery to operate in single-gun or two-gun sections, often alongside an assigned infantry battalion.

Units were trained according to drill manuals written at the end of the Seven Years' War, stressing the tactics used by Frederick the Great of Prussia – lines of tightly arranged men moving in highly regimented maneuvers choreographed to fit at ascending levels of command: company, battalion, and army. Battle consisted of either breaking the opponent's line using artillery and musket fire or, preferably, flanking the enemy's line and then using cavalry to seal the victory. This style of warfare required great discipline from the individual soldier – the discipline to execute

Diagrams of light-infantry formations from the 1817 New Spain manual issued to the Batallón Ligero Provincial de San Luis. Light infantry played an increasingly important role in Royalist armies as a means of countering Patriot guerrillas. Light-infantry units composed a third, or even one half, of the infantry in late-war Royalist armies. (California State Library; photograph by author)

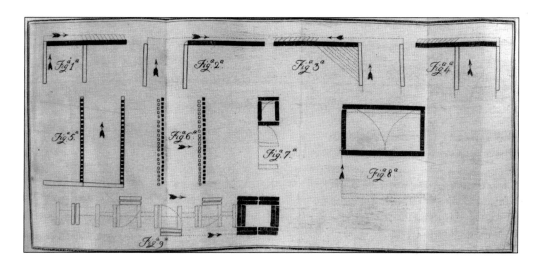

Batalla de Calibio, c. 1846–60, by José María Espinosa (1796–1883). Espinosa was a participant in many early battles, including Calibio on January 15, 1814; his paintings depict the rigid formations and tactics, modeled on those employed by the Prussian Army of the Seven Years' War, that were initially used by both sides. (Casa Museo del 20 de Julio, 1810, Colombia)

highly specialized routines of both moving and firing their weapons, the discipline to maintain their place in the line regardless of danger or opportunity, and the discipline only to act when ordered to do so.

Officers and men began arriving from European Napoleonic battlefields as the war progressed. These men not only brought the painful modernizing lessons learned by the Spanish army, but also French and British doctrines. The use of light infantry increased, fire discipline improved, and more flexible tactical formations were introduced. Cavalry tactics also improved, especially in Río de la Plata, where José de San Martín personally trained a regiment of horse grenadiers in a variety of complex attack maneuvers that made it one of the most effective units in the conflict and equal to any European

regiment. In all cases, adaptations to the geography and cultures affected the armies. In terms of uniforms, sandals and ponchos replaced European shoes and greatcoats, while lances were commonly used, not just by cavalry but by infantry short of muskets.

South America featured several unique types of light cavalry, most notably the Llaneros of New Granada and Gauchos of Río de la Plata. Both were frontier cowboys who tended giant herds of cattle; they were heavily influenced by the vast plains and interaction with native tribes. They relied on almost superhuman horsemanship, personal bravery, an unforgiving code of honor, and a strong attachment to their Caudillo, or leader. Llaneros fought as front-line shock cavalry, while Gauchos fought as guerrillas. In both cases, their feats astounded outside observers and struck terror into their foes.

The wars saw major Indian uprisings in New Spain, Peru, and Upper Peru. Despite the expansive theater of war, these troops were similar in tactics and equipment. Most Indians were equipped with a mixture of clubs, slings, and lances. A small percentage of men, usually regional militia or defectors, were armed with muskets. Men were divided into units based on weapon type, with musketeers and artillery considered the elite of the force. Indian armies were usually described as "masses" or "mobs," indicating they had little formal training and relied upon weight of numbers to overwhelm their opponents. They could sustain heavy casualties in battle, but once broken were impossible to rally or reorganize. Indian armies usually employed artillery, sometimes in greater quantity than any of the regular armies, but the quality of both the guns and crews were low. The Indian armies in Peru were about 15 percent cavalry, but cavalry was less common in New Spain and Upper Peru.

Mercenaries played a limited but vital role. Spain had a long tradition of employing Irish troops and several high-ranking officers were Irishmen. The Patriots made far greater use of foreigners. British and French officers

were a common sight as general's aides and unit commanders, while over 6,000 British and Irish troops enlisted in Bolívar's armies. In New Spain hundreds of American filibusters joined local Patriots in a joint campaign in Texas.

Navies

Naval operations played an important role in the wars. Spain needed command of the sea to maintain communications, trade, and reinforcement, while the Patriots used naval power to isolate Royalist forces and regions, as well as to bring in revenue from prize captures. The navies were small, both in size and class of ships. The majority of ships on both sides were frigates, brigs, and schooners, although a few Spanish ships-of-the-line made limited appearances. Many of the campaigns were conducted in coastal waters or on major rivers. In these campaigns gunboats and flatboats, called *flecheras* in Venezuela, played a prominent role.

Spain's navy had been decimated by over two decades of neglect and defeat. It constantly struggled to field seaworthy ships and lacked the funds to significantly increase

Accion de la Sabana de la Guardia, 1830, by Pedro Pablo Castillo (1780–?). This painting, depicting a battle in 1822, shows much greater tactical sophistication than that shown at Calibio. On the right flank a Patriot infantry unit engages the Royalists in a musket duel, while skirmishers harass the rear and cavalry works around the flank. (Casa de Páez, Venezuela; photograph by José Peña)

La primera Escuadra Nacional, no date, by Álvaro Casanova Zenteno (1857–1939). Chile launched her first naval squadron of four ships in 1818. Under the skilled leadership of Manuel Blanco Encalada (1790–1876) and Thomas Cochrane it went on to play a crucial role in securing Patriot victory by intercepting Spanish reinforcements, capturing Spanish warships, and blockading ports. (Museo Histórico Nacional, Chile; photograph by Marco Benavente)

its strength or even replace losses. The most common roles for Royalist warships were convoy escort and blockade. The Patriot navies also lacked ships, but Great Britain and the United States facilitated private loans and purchases that enabled Río de la Plata and Chile to assemble small fleets. They also made good use of captured Spanish warships, which proved to be the most strategically effective method of changing the balance of power.

The majority of the officers and crews in the Patriot navies were foreign, mostly from Britain and the United States. The most famous sailor during the wars was Thomas Cochrane (1775–1860), the fabled Royal Navy commander turned mercenary, but each of the Patriot navies boasted a talented foreign commander. Río de la Plata had the service of William Brown (1777–1857), born in the United States and a veteran of the Royal Navy, while Venezuela had Luis Brión (1782–1821), a Dutchman from the Curaçao Islands.

Leaders

Considering the small size of the independence-era armies compared to their European counterparts, there was an amazing number of important leaders and commanders. In the course of the wars, however, a few rose to dominance. Studied together, they give a sense of the range of personalities and leadership qualities in both armies.

José María Morelos (1765–1815) was originally a parish priest in southern New Spain. Commissioned into Hidalgo's Patriot army in 1810, he demonstrated an immediate grasp of all aspects of military command, from training to field tactics. He had read the works of Frederick the Great and adapted them to fit his peasant soldiers, stressing discipline and unquestioning obedience to orders. Despite being swamped with volunteers, Morelos refused to accept more recruits than he could properly feed, train, and equip. To the rest he explained that their duty was to return home and

Morelos, from *El Libro Rojo*, 1870, by Vicente Riva Palacio (1832–96) and Manuel Payno (1810–94). When Morelos was captured in 1815 he was humiliated by both Church and government authorities. His final humiliation was being shot in the back by his firing squad, a common fate for rebel leaders. (Anne S.K. Brown Collection; photograph by René Chartrand)

produce food, equipment and supplies for the army. Morelos proved himself an adept battlefield commander, regularly besting professionally trained officers using a mix of guerrilla warfare and the standard tactics of the day. Politically, Morelos combined Enlightenment principles with his devout Catholic faith in seeking to forge a new and just society. He was a true citizen-soldier.

Simón Bolívar (1783–1830) was a wealthy Creole from one of the best families in Venezuela. He spent his youth in Europe, traveling and being educated by a personal tutor. Inspired by the French Revolution, he is said to have shouted an oath to liberate Venezuela from a mountaintop in Italy. Whether prompted by idealistic passion or narcissistic megalomania, the gesture encapsulated the essence of Bolívar, who made himself the living embodiment of the revolution. Bolívar was bored by the day-to-day tasks of both military and governmental routine. As a result, his armies suffered grievously due to poor planning and logistics, but it was of little concern to Bolívar; all that mattered was the revolution and his glory. Bolívar was highly charismatic and exceptionally cunning. He possessed an uncanny ability to read a situation, which allowed him to frequently outmaneuver both political and military foes.

José de San Martín (1778–1850) was a professional soldier with 22 years of military experience when he joined the Patriot army in Buenos Aires. He was a meticulous organizer who despised mobs or rabble and refused to allow such in his army. An excellent drillmaster, San Martín would personally train a section of soldiers who then trained their own sections. The same applied to officers, who were handpicked and personally schooled in the latest tactics. The support elements of his army received the same attention and were second to none. San Martín was the only Patriot general to

San Martín, 1818, by José Gil de Castro (1785–1841). San Martín was a career officer in the Spanish Army who returned to his native Buenos Aires in 1812. He led Patriot armies in the liberation of Chile and Peru. (Museo Histórico Nacional, Argentina)

Paso de los Andes, 1911, by Tito Salas (1887–1974).
Few events better illustrate the differences between
Bolívar and San Martín than their famed crossings of
the Andes. Bolívar relied on his men's willpower and
endurance; San Martín on meticulous planning and
logistics. (Palacio Federal Legislativo, Venezuela)

formulate and implement a consistent,
coherent grand strategy for winning the war.
The downside of his regimented approach
was that San Martín did not improvise well
and missed several opportunities to exploit
a situation or strike a critical blow.

José Tomás Boves (1782–1814) was a
Spanish merchant who settled in the remote
town of Calabozo on the edge of the vast
plains of southern Venezuela. In the early
days of the war a Creole officer tortured him,
murdered his assistant, and burned his
business to the ground. His desire for
revenge led him to the Royalist banner.
Outside a brief stint in the Spanish navy
he had no military experience, but rose to
leadership through his physical prowess and
reputation as an honest businessman who

cared nothing for caste. Strategically and tactically clueless, Boves simply went to where the enemy was and led the charge into them. Defeat did not deter him and victory did not make him complacent. Boves made maximum use of his men's frontier ferocity and outlaw nature, actively encouraging plunder, rape, and murder.

Pablo Morillo (1775–1837) joined the Spanish army at the age of 12, rising through the ranks to become a general. He made his fame during the Peninsular War, where he led guerrilla and regular units, defeated the French commander Marshal Michel Ney in 1809, and commanded one of the few Spanish divisions integrated directly into Wellington's army. Morillo arrived in Venezuela in 1815 at the head of a 12,000-man Spanish army espousing a policy of reconciliation. He abandoned this policy in 1816 after the Patriot commander on Margarita Island dishonored his vow of submission and renewed hostilities. Despite being portrayed as a psychopathic monster by Patriot propaganda, Morillo was less violent than almost any of the Venezuelan generals on either side, and eventually concluded a regularization of the war with Bolívar in 1820. A talented soldier who consistently made do with what he had, Morillo privately came to the conclusion that the war was unwinnable but remained steadfastly committed to carrying out his orders to the best of his abilities.

Loyal revolutionaries

The key event that triggered colonial independence was the French invasion of Spain in 1808. Spain had been allied with France since 1796. In early 1808 Napoleon Bonaparte, Emperor of France, decided to depose the Spanish King Charles IV and his heir Ferdinand VII and install a member of his own family on the throne. In a series of treacherous diplomatic moves he easily outwitted Charles and Ferdinand. Meanwhile, 100,000 French soldiers occupied Spain. On May 2, 1808 riots broke out in Madrid, signaling the beginning of

Retrato de Fernando VII con manto real, 1814, by Francisco Goya (1746–1828). Beginning and ending his reign in a dispute over royal succession and constantly struggling against efforts to introduce representative government, Ferdinand VII's rule was marked by disastrous civil wars, including the colonial rebellions, that permanently crippled Spain's power. (Museo Nacional del Prado, Spain)

Spanish resistance to the French occupation. Local resistance turned into full-scale war as French rule was overwhelmingly rejected all across the country. Regional ruling councils, called juntas, formed across Spain to fill the governmental vacuum. The juntas argued that in the absence of the king legitimate government devolved to the local level. Leadership coalesced around the self-styled Supreme Central and Governmental Junta of Spain and the Indies in Seville (often called the Supreme Junta or Seville Junta for brevity), which became the de facto national government in 1809. When Seville fell to the French in 1810 the junta disbanded, and what remained of national government fled to the nearby city of Cádiz.

As news of the invasion reached Spain's colonies, so did the example of the juntas. To some the idea made sense – the colonies should follow the Spanish example and form juntas to rule until the return of Ferdinand VII, wistfully nicknamed "The Desired One." Others argued that the junta model made no sense. The colonies still had properly sanctioned royal authorities in the persons of the governing viceroys and administrators. These officials made juntas irrelevant at best and seditious at worst. In general terms this divided the sides into two camps – Patriots, those in favor of juntas, and Royalists, those in favor of the existing order.

New Spain

In New Spain the Patriot banner fell to a radicalized parish priest named Father Miguel Hidalgo y Costilla (1753–1811). A passionate student of the Enlightenment, Hidalgo held salon-style gatherings in his small parish town of Dolores, where he

discussed topics like popular sovereignty and economic empowerment for Mestizos and Indians. In March 1810 Hidalgo was approached by a local militia officer, Ignacio Allende (1769–1811), with a proposition to join a Creole conspiracy to overthrow the Peninsulares in New Spain. A previous attempt in late 1808 by Creoles to convince the viceroy to form a junta and recognize New Spain as an autonomous kingdom failed, as Absolutists had taken the extraordinary step of unilaterally replacing the viceroy in the name of retaining the viceregal system. The conspirators thought the time was ripe to try again. Although Hidalgo's republican sentiments worried the conspirators, they believed his standing among the lower classes was vital to success. In September one of the conspirators confessed the scheme to Royalist authorities. Hidalgo and Allende received word of the betrayal on the night of September 15, 1810. At dawn on September 16, Hidalgo stepped into the crowded central market of Dolores and urged the crowd to take up arms, seize their rightful lands, and depose the Peninsulares, all in the name of Ferdinand VII and the Virgin of Guadalupe. His speech has become immortalized as the "Grito de Dolores" ("Cry of Dolores").

Carlos IV y su hijo Fernando reunidos con Napoleón en Bayona, no date, artist unknown. Napoleon Bonaparte cleverly tricked Charles IV and his son Ferdinand VII into mutually abdicating the Spanish throne. Napoleon named his brother Joseph king of Spain, igniting war in both Spain and the colonies. (Biblioteca de la Alianza Francesa Central de Buenos Aires)

The original plan was for Allende to lead militia troops in a limited campaign against a narrow swath of viceregal authority. Hidalgo's role was to keep the masses supportive but under control. Instead, Hidalgo paraded humiliated Peninsulares before the crowd and initiated a peasant march towards Guanajuato, a major mining city and Royalist administrative center. By the time they arrived in Guanajuato, Allende had gathered 100 militiamen, but Hidalgo had attracted a mob of 25,000, fueled by religious fervor, generations of exploitation, and recent food shortages. The local Royalist commander gathered his troops and the terrified whites of the city inside the local granary, an ironic choice given the mob's grievances. The granary was the next best thing to a fortress and the Royalists killed hundreds as the Patriots stormed the walls, but the sheer mass of Patriots carried the day. After five hours the granary fell. The mob killed everyone inside, combatants and

Spanish America in 1807

UNITED STATES

ATLANTIC OCEAN

San Francisco

St. Louis

Santa Fe

San Diego

VICEROYALTY OF NEW SPAIN

Bexar

HAVANA

MEXICO CITY

Acapulco

HAITI   SAN JUAN

BELIZE   JAMAICA   SANTO DOMINGO

GUATEMALA CITY

Granada

Coro   CARACAS

Cartagena   TRINIDAD

Angostura   **CAPTAINCY** **DEMERARA**

GENERAL OF   Demerara

BOGOTÁ   **VENEZUELA**   **FRENCH GUIANA**

VICEROYALTY   **SURINAM**

OF NEW

GRANADA

QUITO

PACIFIC

OCEAN

VICEROYALTY   B R A Z I L

OF PERU

Callao

LIMA

Cuzco

La Paz

UPPER PERU

Chuquisaca

PARAGUAY   RÍO DE JANEIRO

Asunción

SANTIAGO   BANDA ORIENTAL

BUENOS AIRES   Montevideo

VICEROYALTY

OF RÍO DE

LA PLATA

	Captaincy General of Guatemala
	Captaincy General of Cuba
	Captaincy General of Santo Domingo
	Captaincy General of Puerto Rico
	Royal Audience of Quito
	Captaincy General of Chile
	British possessions
	French possessions
	Dutch possessions

0   Miles   1,500

0   Kilometers   3,000

non-combatants alike. As news of the massacre spread, almost the entire Creole population joined with the Peninsulares, while the lower classes flocked to Hidalgo's banner.

In contrast to Hidalgo's uprising, the islands of Cuba and Puerto Rico, as well as the regions of Santo Domingo and Central America, remained firmly in Royalist control. This was due to geographic isolation, strong garrisons, and fear of slave uprisings leading to race wars. Except for some limited fighting in Panama, these regions remained peaceful. Central America declared independence in 1821 while Santo Domingo was occupied by Haiti in 1822. Cuba and Puerto Rico remained Royalist and served as important Spanish bases throughout the conflict.

New Granada

Despite having limited resources, New Granada's viceroy, Antonio José Amar y Borbón, vigorously opposed the junta movement. When he heard of a junta forming in Quito in August 1809, he dispatched troops to restore order. In October Amar had the ringleaders of a pro-junta conspiracy in Bogotá imprisoned while the militia patrolled the streets. Despite these efforts, news of the collapse of the Seville junta renewed the push for autonomous government. Cartagena, the viceroyalty's major port, formed a junta on June 14, 1810. Others followed and on July 20, with a mob threatening his life, Amar allowed a junta in Bogotá itself. Five days later he was deposed.

The new juntas immediately set upon each other. The key issue was whether the juntas should operate as a loose confederation or under strong, centralized leadership. A congress was called with the intent of solving the question. Most of the country agreed to organize as a series of independent but confederated provincial states called the United Provinces of New Granada. Each state pursued its own laws and policies in domestic matters while a

congress at Tunja oversaw and coordinated policies that affected the whole. Bogotá rejected this solution, insisting that only a strong central government could resist Spain. Bogotá formed its own state called Cundinamarca, which was the name of the province around the city. None of the provinces trusted each other, with particularly harsh condemnations leveled against Antonio Nariño, a lifelong revolutionary who had risen to become the dictator-president of Cundinamarca. Meanwhile, Royalist forces remained in control of key areas, including Popayán and Pasto in the south and Santa Marta, near Cartagena, in the north.

Venezuela was a captaincy general of New Granada. Captaincies general were technically part of the larger viceroyalties but were autonomously administered. A junta was formed in Caracas, the capital, on April 18, 1810 and was quickly joined by most of the provinces. The provinces of Guayana and Maracaibo, in the eastern and western portions of the country respectively, remained Royalist. The city of Coro, which was part of Caracas province, also remained Royalist. When the Caracas junta sent representatives to Coro, the governor, José Ceballos, had them arrested. The junta declared Ceballos an agent of France and assembled an army of 4,000 men under Marquis Francisco Rodríguez del Toro to take Coro. Although Ceballos could only muster 1,200 men, half of them armed with spears and bows, he defeated Toro on the outskirts of Coro on November 28, 1810.

In Caracas a congress was convened to determine the future government. Radical voices led by Francisco de Miranda and his protégé, Simón Bolívar, both recently returned from overseas, demanded full independence. They carried the day and the new Venezuelan Republic declared independence on July 5, 1811. Royalists immediately rebelled in Caracas and Valencia. The Caracas disturbance was easily put down but Valencia held out for a month against Republican forces, falling to Miranda on August 11, 1811.

Río de la Plata

News of the French invasion reached Buenos
Aires at a momentous time. Río de la Plata
had recently defeated two separate British
expeditions during which an open council
had stripped the viceroy of power – an
unprecedented and shocking expression of
local strength. The council named Santiago
de Liniers, a Frenchman in Spanish service
who had fought bravely against the British,
as viceroy. Peninsulares, wishing a return to
the old order, attempted a coup against
Liniers on January 1, 1809 but were defeated
by Creole factions. Nearby Montevideo, seat
for the Banda Oriental province of Río de la
Plata, refused to recognize Liniers and split
off under its own governor.

In June 1809 Baltasar Hidalgo de Cisneros
(1755–1829) was sent by the Seville Junta
for the express purpose of invalidating
Buenos Aires' insubordination. Upon
Cisneros' arrival Liniers immediately
relinquished office. Cisneros restored order
in Buenos Aires even as new challenges arose
in Upper Peru. Juntas formed in Chuquisaca
on May 25, 1809 and La Paz on July 16. In
October Cisneros dispatched 1,000 men

*Cabildo Abierto 22 de mayo, 1910, by Pedro Subercaseaux
(1880–1956). Open councils, traditional gatherings of
locally influential citizens that decided important matters,
declared juntas across the colonies to rule until
Ferdinand VII regained the throne. The new juntas
were immediately pitted against the existing Spanish
authorities, setting the stage for war. (Museo Histórico
Nacional, Argentina)*

under Vicente Nieto to restore order
in Chuquisaca while Abascal's 5,000
Peruvians pacified La Paz. In putting
down the Chuquisaca rebellion, Cisneros
inadvertently weakened his hand in Buenos
Aires. The troops sent to Upper Peru were
drawn from the small Spanish regular army
garrison, leaving the Creole militia in a
dominant position.

On May 13, 1810 a British ship arrived in
Montevideo with news that the Seville Junta
had disbanded and what was left of Spanish
authority was holed up in Cádiz. The Creoles
in Buenos Aires demanded an open council,
stacked with their own delegates. On
May 25, 1810 the council deposed Cisneros,
declared a junta in his place, and presumed
national leadership over all of Río de la Plata
– despite the fact that none of the other
regions had been invited to the council.

Peru

Peru stayed firmly under the Royalist control of its viceroy, José Fernando de Abascal y Sousa. Abascal was a highly competent administrator who established Peru as the bulwark for Royalist power in South America throughout the conflict. Peru's Creoles had many reasons to stay attached to the old order, but two dominated: commercial rivalry with Buenos Aires, particularly over control of the silver-producing province of Upper Peru, and memories of the Túpac Amaru rebellion in 1780.

Abascal was a strong, Conservative monarchist. He viewed any call for regional representation as outright rebellion. When the 1812 Constitution was proclaimed he implemented it half-heartedly at best, looking forward to the full restoration of "The Desired One." Abascal faced a more subtle challenge in dealing with Ferdinand's sister, Carlotta. Carlotta was Queen of Portugal, living in exile with the rest of the Portuguese royal family in Brazil. Carlotta offered to rule the colonies as Princess Regent until Ferdinand's restoration. Although this appeared to provide an acceptable solution and was even supported by some Patriots, Abascal recognized the strategic threat posed by establishing any Portuguese claim over Spanish colonies. Abascal diplomatically stalled the proposal. His patience paid off when the Portuguese monarch, John VI, forbade his wife the right to travel, thereby scuttling the issue. Meanwhile, Abascal organized expeditions to troubled regions, even those technically outside his jurisdiction. He sent 5,000 men under José Manuel de Goyeneche to put down a junta in La Paz and 500 men to reinforce a 2,000-man Royalist army operating against Quito.

The Spanish reaction

News of the junta uprisings reached Spain at its lowest point in the war with France. Seville had fallen in early 1810 and the Supreme Junta had fled to Cádiz, the last free city in the country. The Supreme Junta then dissolved itself and formed a five-man council called the Council of Regency of Spain and the Indies. The Regency in turn called for a national assembly, dubbed the Cortes. In the desperate need to gather every resource against the French, the Seville Junta had recognized the colonies as an integral part of Spain itself – "a crown with two pillars" (Chasteen 2008: 78) – and the Regency invited American representatives to take part in the deliberations of the Cortes, foremost of which was writing a new national constitution. Even as the American delegates fought for greater autonomy in the new constitution, they sought to reassure the Spanish that the colonial disturbances were the expressions of a misguided few, not signs of widespread rebellion. Many Spanish members of the Cortes sympathized with the colonists' grievances even as they sought to perpetuate their own dominance. They were convinced their work would end the uprisings and usher in a new era of harmony. On March 19, 1812 the Cortes triumphantly unveiled the 1812 Constitution, an enlightened document that established a limited monarchy under parliamentary control, expanded the rights of private property, asserted individual liberty, and shifted the balance of power from the old nobility to the commercial class – all points that should have appealed to disgruntled Creoles. The Cádiz government also liberalized trade, ended Indian tributes, and ended restrictions on agricultural and industrial production. Certain they had addressed the uprisings, the Spanish even offered amnesty for the rebels who, they assumed, would immediately see their error and lay down arms.

One powerful group, however, was not so certain. Cádiz's merchants had been the primary beneficiaries of the monopolistic trade system and had seen their revenues plummet with the outbreak of colonial rebellion. They believed the only way the rebels would lay down arms was if they were compelled to do so by force. Unfortunately,

La promulgación de la Constitución de 1812, 1912, by Salvador Viniegra (1862–1915). Spanish liberals expected the 1812 Constitution to diffuse the colonial uprisings and usher in a new era of advancement for all of Spain. (Museo de las Cortes de Cádiz)

the army was busy fighting the French and the navy had been decimated by years of war with Britain and neglect at home. Their solution was to form the Comision de Reemplazos ("Commission of Replacements") in September 1811 to independently fund, raise, and equip military expeditions to the colonies. While the Comision was technically under governmental supervision, it answered to the merchants and guilds of the city. The Comision wielded great power and served as the primary organizational entity, even after Ferdinand was restored to the throne in 1814. Over the course of the war, the Comision was involved in outfitting 30 expeditions that sent over 47,000 regular Spanish soldiers to the Americas.

La Firma del Acta de la Independencia, 1838, by Juan Lovera (1776–1841). The various colonial juntas initially swore fealty to Ferdinand VII. However, radical voices moved toward openly declaring independence within a matter of months. (Congreso Nacional de Venezuela)

"War to the Death"

New Spain

The massacre of whites at Guanajuato was a seminal event in the war in New Spain. It caused a rift between the main Patriot leaders, Miguel Hidalgo and Ignacio Allende. Allende was incensed by the indiscipline and savagery displayed by Hidalgo's Indians. He feared the massacre threatened the entire revolution, both by its simple immorality and also because it would drive Creoles into the Royalist camp. Hidalgo rationalized that the Spanish had been pillaging and massacring the Indians for 300 years and some retribution was unavoidable. Hidalgo also knew a two-year drought had brought the peasants to the point of desperation. There was no money to pay them or supplies to feed them – plunder was the only way to keep them in the field. Both men were correct. As word of the massacre filtered back to Mexico City the uniform reaction was horror, evoking the spectre of a Haitian-style race war. Open support for the Patriots vanished. At the same time Hidalgo's ranks swelled from 25,000 to 80,000 as Indians saw an outlet for their longstanding anger and misery, while Allende added over 2,000 trained militiamen as the Royalist garrison of Valladolid defected.

By coincidence a new viceroy, Francisco Javier Venegas, arrived in New Spain two days before the "Grito de Dolores." Venegas was an experienced officer and administrator. He reacted swiftly, concentrating Royalist garrisons and raising new units. He enlisted the Church, which excommunicated Hidalgo and preached resistance to the Patriots' unholy rebellion. Most importantly, he had two determined field commanders: Lieutenant Colonel Torcuato Trujillo and Brigadier General Félix Calleja. Both men were resolute, tactically proficient, and merciless.

Trujillo was given command of 7,000 men, mostly untested militia, around Mexico City. Despite being outnumbered more than ten to one, Trujillo confronted Hidalgo on October 30, 1810 at the battle of Monte de las Cruces. The battle raged all day. Allende's militiamen surrounded Trujillo while Hidalgo's peasants made continual frontal assaults. Trujillo lost a third of his army but escaped back to Mexico City. The Patriots lost a stunning 40,000 men, most of whom probably simply fled the battlefield.

The Patriots reached Mexico City on November 1, 1810. Venegas fortified the city as best he could: barricading streets, stationing troops at key points, and even arming some slaves. Venegas found his own

Viceroy Calleja, c. 1820, artist unknown. Félix Calleja was a Spanish officer who made his name as a frontier fighter against Indians and American filibusters. His combat experience placed him in the forefront of Royalist commanders and he eventually became viceroy of New Spain. (Museo Nacional de Historia, Mexico; photograph by René Chartrand)

Marian symbol, the Virgin of Los Remedios, to counter the Patriots' Virgin of Guadalupe. The cathedral of Mexico City was filled with women praying to be spared the ravages of Hidalgo's horde. Instead of initiating the anticipated battle, however, Hidalgo sent a representative to demand the city's surrender. Venegas refused and after several

Hidalgo, from *El Libro Rojo*, 1870, by Vicente Riva Palacio (1832–96) and Manuel Payno (1810–94). Miguel Hidalgo was an Enlightenment-influenced village priest, beloved by the lower castes. Originally intended to play a supporting role, he became commander of the Patriot army in New Spain and father of Mexican independence. (Anne S.K. Brown Collection; photograph by René Chartrand)

tense days Hidalgo withdrew. Allende was furious and whatever shred of respect still existed between the two Patriot leaders was lost. Calleja's army easily routed the retreating Patriots at Aculco on November 7. Hidalgo and Allende split during the retreat, with Allende returning to Guanajuato, which Calleja retook in another Patriot rout on November 24. For the next three days Calleja publicly executed Patriot prisoners and collaborators at the site of the massacre two months before – only one episode in a tit-for-tat series of atrocities and reprisals that became a hallmark of the wars of independence.

Hidalgo spent the rest of 1810 in Guadalajara, rebuilding his army and attempting to regain the initiative. To maintain peasant support he continued to execute Peninsulares, declared land and tax reform, and abolished slavery. By the beginning of 1811 he had 80,000 men but only 200 muskets. Allende rejoined the army but realized it was not battleworthy. He advised dispersing the army and fighting a guerrilla campaign. Hidalgo disagreed, and, on hearing news that Calleja's Royalists were approaching, marched to meet them. The Patriots took up position at Calderón Bridge, a natural chokepoint on Calleja's route. Calleja attacked on January 17, 1811. The battle raged for six hours before a stray grenade blew up a Patriot ammunition wagon, starting a wildfire that burned across the Patriot lines. The Patriots fled hopelessly in all directions.

After the defeat Patriot leadership scattered, most heading north to join Patriots in Texas or even to regroup in the United States. Hidalgo and Allende were captured, tried, and executed. Before his death Hidalgo issued an astonishing confession. He admitted acting no better than "a common criminal" and mourned the "evil" he had unleashed on the country. Some claim this was a heartfelt repentance, others that it was a forged document. Regardless, Venegas responded by displaying Hidalgo's head at the granary at Guanajuato, where it hung until 1821.

Hidalgo's defeat did not end the revolution. Hidalgo had dispatched several lieutenants to take the struggle to other regions of New Spain. The most important of these was José María Morelos. Like Hidalgo, Morelos was a well-read, politically progressive parish priest dedicated to improving the conditions of the average peasant. Despite his lack of military experience, Hidalgo made him an officer in October 1810. Morelos was given 20 men and the task of taking the key Pacific port of Acapulco. It was an absurd order given the strength of the fortified city, but Morelos immediately showed his exceptional abilities.

He recruited a limited number of men and made sure they were well armed and trained according to the tactics of Frederick the Great. Plunder was forbidden and even minor instances of disobedience were grounds for capital punishment. In battle, Morelos showed capabilities beyond anything previously seen in the viceroyalty. Over the course of 1811 he won 22 engagements against three Royalist armies. In the process, he identified and promoted talented officers to lead his ever-growing army. By the end of the year he had 9,000 men in three divisions and controlled most of the southwestern coastal region. However, he failed to take Acapulco, a fact that haunted him.

Venegas eyed Morelos' success with alarm. By the end of 1811, the Patriots controlled almost all the country to the south and west of Mexico City. Another Patriot leader, Ignacio López Rayón, had even installed a functioning rebel government in the town of Zitácuaro. Venegas gave Calleja 5,000 men and orders to restore control. On January 2, 1812 Calleja attacked Rayón's 20,000 peasants. Although Calleja lost 2,000 men, he completely destroyed the Patriot army and burned Zitácuaro to the ground.

In early February Morelos occupied Cuautla with over 4,000 troops. Calleja, reinforced after Zitácuaro, approached the city on February 17 with 7,000 men. Twice repulsed trying to storm the city, Calleja imposed a ten-week siege. The Patriots were reduced to eating rats and tree bark, but Morelos refused to surrender. Their provisions exhausted, Morelos' army, accompanied by the civilian population, stole through the Royalist lines during the predawn hours of May 2. Following the course of a riverbed they eluded the Royalist pickets, but were eventually discovered and annihilated. Morelos escaped, but over 3,000 Patriots were killed.

Morelos quickly recovered from his defeat and began a new offensive, this time around the town of Oaxaca. He captured several cities including Huajuapan, which fell after a 111-day siege. During 1812 Morelos received

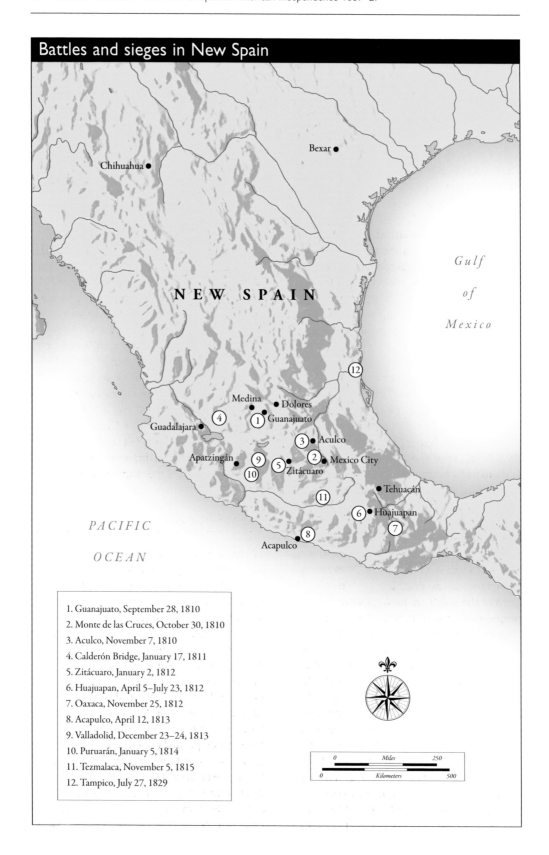

Battles and sieges in New Spain

Bexar

Chihuahua

Gulf

of

Mexico

NEW SPAIN

12

Medina   Dolores

Guadalajara   4   1 Guanajuato

3 Aculco

Apatzingán   9   5   2 Mexico City

10   Zitácuaro

11   Tehuacán

6 Huajuapan

PACIFIC   7

OCEAN   8

Acapulco

1. Guanajuato, September 28, 1810

2. Monte de las Cruces, October 30, 1810

3. Aculco, November 7, 1810

4. Calderón Bridge, January 17, 1811

5. Zitácuaro, January 2, 1812

6. Huajuapan, April 5–July 23, 1812

7. Oaxaca, November 25, 1812

8. Acapulco, April 12, 1813

9. Valladolid, December 23–24, 1813

10. Puruarán, January 5, 1814

11. Tezmalaca, November 5, 1815

12. Tampico, July 27, 1829

| 0 | Miles | 250 |
| 0 | Kilometers | 500 |

increasing support from Creoles in Mexico City, including an effective spy network that sent a constant stream of high-level intelligence. When Oaxaca fell in November, the Creoles urged him to attack Mexico City. The city was in a deplorable state, with a collapsed economy and war-weary populace in the grip of a horrific yellow-fever pandemic, which eventually killed 20,000. Venegas lost all support and Calleja replaced him in March 1813. Instead of striking the final blow while the Royalists were at their lowest ebb, Morelos returned to Acapulco. The city fell in August 1813 after a five-month siege, but by then it was too late. Calleja not only consolidated control in Mexico City, but defeated several smaller insurgent groups. Morelos, on the other hand, became bogged down establishing a new government. A congress was formed and independence declared on November 6. In December Morelos returned to the field, but was defeated at Valladolid on December 23–24. This defeat was due to a young Royalist colonel named Agustín de Iturbide, who, while reconnoitering the Patriot lines with 350 men, saw a weakness and ordered an attack so reckless it shocked the Patriots, who broke and fled.

Morelos was again defeated and nearly captured at Puruarán on January 5, 1814. The newly formed congress, encouraged by Rayón, effectively stripped him of command. Congress itself was attacked on February 24 and scattered. The Patriots lost all their gains in the south, including Oaxaca and Acapulco. As defeats mounted, the Patriots fractured into squabbling bands under independent chieftains who began fighting among themselves. Congress spent 1814 and 1815 seeking a safe base to renew hostilities. In October they ordered Morelos to escort them to Tehuacán, on the Gulf of Mexico. Morelos had about 1,000 men, whose quality was a shadow of the meticulously trained warriors of 1812. After a month expertly guiding Congress through Royalist territory, Morelos was eventually brought to battle at Tezmalaca on November 5, 1815. Morelos was captured fighting a desperate rearguard action that allowed Congress to escape. Morelos was subjected to a series of humiliations, first by the Inquisition and then by the royal authorities. He was executed on December 22, 1815.

Morelos' defeat was, in many ways, the defeat of the revolution in New Spain. Insurgent chiefs, most notably Vicente Guerrero (1782–1831), continued the fight, but none threatened Spanish rule on more than a local scale. On the Royalist side, Calleja's harsh methods and high taxes quickly fell out of favor. He was replaced in 1816 by Juan Ruiz de Apodaca (1754–1835). Apodaca pursued more conciliatory policies, including an amnesty that caused thousands of Patriots to lay down their arms. A highly anticipated expedition from New Orleans led by Francisco Xavier Mina (1789–1817), an exiled Spanish Liberal and guerrilla hero of the Peninsular War, landed in March 1817 but failed to elicit support. Mina was captured and executed in October 1817. The war devolved into a series of territorial sweeps by demoralized Royalists hunting down bands of desperate Patriots, who were often little more than highway bandits. Mostly, both sides were simply exhausted.

New Granada

When Cartagena and Venezuela declared independence, Spain responded by sending the handful of available regulars to the region. Three Spanish companies landed at Santa Marta, where Royalists waged a limited campaign against Cartagena, while Frigate Captain Juan Domingo de Monteverde landed with a company of marines at Coro. Monteverde, reinforced with a handful of local militia, made a raid against the nearby town of Siquisique on March 17, 1812. On his approach the Patriot garrison defected. Monteverde pressed on and soon had over 1,500 men. To address the Royalist threat, Miranda was named generalissimo and dictator on March 25. The next day an earthquake devastated central Venezuela. Approximately 10,000 people died in Caracas

José María Morelos, c. 1815. Morelos was a village priest who joined Hidalgo's rebellion in 1810. He proved a capable leader, fielding a disciplined army and shaping the Constitution of Apatzingán in 1814. (Museo Nacional de Historia, Mexico; photograph by René Chartrand)

alone. Royalist clergy declared the earthquake God's judgment on a rebellious people.

As Miranda organized his army in the ruined capital, Monteverde continued his advance. The two armies faced off between Valencia and La Victoria in May and June. Miranda had 5,000 men, Monteverde 3,000. Miranda defeated Monteverde in two battles at La Victoria, on June 20 and June 29, but refused to pursue the defeated Royalists. On July 2 word arrived that Bolívar had lost the strategic port of La Puerta to an uprising of Royalist prisoners. Patriot morale collapsed. Miranda concluded the campaign was lost and negotiated surrender. He attempted to escape on board a British vessel, but was apprehended by Bolívar and handed over to the Royalists. Bolívar himself escaped to Cartagena. Miranda died in a Spanish prison in 1816.

In Quito a new Patriot junta had arisen in October 1811. In 1812 it sent forces against Pasto to the north and Cuenca to the south. Both expeditions ended in failure, and Royalist forces from Guayaquil and Cuenca, reinforced by troops from Lima, pressed

northwards. The Patriots were crushed on November 7, 1812 at El Panecillo, a prominent hill in Quito. The Royalists continued north, reinforcing Pasto and taking nearby Popayán, thereby securing southern New Granada.

In March 1812 Antonio Nariño, lead Centralist advocate, sent a small division against the Federalist Congress in Tunja. Antonio Baraya, commander of the expedition, defected to Congress on May 25. Nariño assembled more troops, but failed to bring the United Provinces forces to battle. Baraya, reinforced with United Provinces troops, marched on Bogotá in December. Nariño offered conditional surrender, including his own exile, but Baraya refused. After several skirmishes Baraya launched a full assault on January 9, 1813. Heavily outnumbered, Nariño conducted a skillful defense around the city square and routed Baraya's army. Nariño pardoned Baraya and formed a tenuous alliance with the United Provinces.

Upon arriving in Cartagena, Bolívar offered his services to the Congress of the United Provinces. He was given 70 men and a garrison post on the Magdalena River. Without awaiting authorization Bolívar initiated a campaign upriver on December 21, 1812. In two weeks he had cleared the river and taken Ocuña, at the foot of the Andes Mountains. After defeating a key Royalist garrison at Cúcuta on February 28, 1813 Bolívar paused to gather reinforcements and get Congressional approval for his real project – a drive on Caracas. The offensive resumed in June. With only 1,500 men, Bolívar based his strategy on speed and terror.

On June 15 Bolívar issued a "War to the Death" decree that ordered the extermination of all Spaniards who did not actively support the revolution. "War to the Death" marked a deliberate rejection of the norms of civilized warfare in pursuit of a specific political goal – splitting Royalist Creoles from Peninsulares. Rafael Urdaneta, one of Bolívar's longest-serving and most trusted generals, explained Bolívar's chilling logic:

Spaniards, knowing they would find certain death, would be cowed, as actually happened; and the Creoles would flock to Bolívar's arms, as it was necessary they should. The result, the occupation of Caracas, fully justified the measure (Madariaga 1952: 200).

Bolívar quickly swept forward, winning several small battles on an inexorable march to the capital. Monteverde, with the last available Royalist troops, retreated to the fortress at Puerto Cabello. Bolívar entered Caracas on August 7, 1813 and was shortly thereafter proclaimed "The Liberator" – a title he clung to until his death.

Once in Caracas, Bolívar found the strategic situation reversed. Large areas of the country were still under Royalist control and those armies had freedom of movement, while the need to protect the capital forced him onto the defensive: 1,000 Spanish regulars arrived to reinforce Monteverde at Puerto Cabello, Ceballos marched south from Coro to unite with a division from the Llanos, as the vast plains region of southern Venezuela were known, and another army of 2,500 Llaneros was forming under José Tomás Boves. Bolívar sent smaller columns against Monteverde and Boves while he attacked Ceballos. The column sent against Boves, led by a talented but bloodthirsty colonel named Vicente Campo Elías, won an overwhelming victory at Mosquiteros on October 14, 1813. Only Boves and 18 men escaped. Campo Elías followed up by massacring civilians in Calabozo, Boves' adopted hometown. The Llaneros were so outraged that in a matter of weeks Boves had formed an even larger army. Bolívar, meanwhile, defeated the Royalists at the battle of Araure on December 5, personally leading a key cavalry charge that secured the victory.

Nariño spent most of 1813 dealing with the political aftermath of his ill-conceived civil war. In September he finally left Bogotá at the head of a 1,500-man division to deal with the surging Royalist forces in southern New Granada. He came into contact with the Royalists at Alto Palace on December 30, where his advance guard forced its way across a difficult river barrier. He defeated 2,000 Royalists at the battle of Calibio on January 15, 1814, securing Popayán, and drove to the gates of Pasto, where he was captured several days after the bloody battle of Tacines on May 9. The Patriot army dissolved and the Royalists regained their losses. Despite demands for Nariño's execution, the Royalist commander, Melchor Aymerich, sent him to prison in Spain.

Like Nariño, Bolívar had rivals in the Patriot camp. His main rival was Santiago Mariño, who, along with his talented Mulatto lieutenant, Manuel Piar, had secured the province of Cumaná in eastern Venezuela. When Bolívar occupied Caracas, he declared the formation of the Second Venezuelan Republic with himself as dictator. Mariño refused to subordinate himself to Bolívar or to help him throughout the latter half of 1813. At the beginning of 1814, however, Mariño had a change of heart and marched west with 4,000 men.

The reinforcements could not arrive quickly enough. Almost as soon as the Royalists were defeated at Araure, Boves appeared with another army, this time over 7,000 strong. Boves defeated Campo Elías at La Puerta on February 3, 1814 but was wounded. Boves' lieutenant, Francisco Morales, was in turn defeated at La Victoria on February 12. It was a brief respite as Boves recovered and led the army to Bolívar's hometown of San Mateo, where Bolívar had 2,100 entrenched troops. There were two major battles, one on February 28, the other on March 25. Bolívar won both battles and on news of Mariño's arrival Boves, his army reduced to 3,000 men, broke off the siege. Mariño finished the triumph by defeating Boves at the battle of Bocachica on March 31.

Like a hydra, the defeat of one Royalist army only led to the rise of another. This time 5,000 troops from Coro and other Royalist detachments were pressing on Valencia. Bolívar, with 6,000 men, defeated them at Carabobo on May 28. Boves, however, had reformed his scattered army and delivered a crushing defeat on Bolívar at La Puerta on June 15. With only 1,100 men remaining and no chance of defending

Battles and sieges in New Granada

1. Coro, November 28, 1810
2. Valencia, July 5–August 11, 1811
3. First battle of La Victoria, June 20, 1812
4. Second battle of La Victoria, June 29, 1812
5. El Panecillo, November 7, 1812
6. Bogotá, January 9, 1813
7. Cúcuta, February 28, 1813
8. Mosquiteros, October 14, 1813
9. Araure, December 5, 1813
10. Alto Palace, December 30, 1813
11. Calibio, January 15, 1814
12. First battle of La Puerta, February 3, 1814
13. First battle of San Mateo, February 28, 1814
14. Second battle of San Mateo, March 25, 1814
15. Bocachica, March 31, 1814
16. Tacines, May 9, 1814
17. First battle of Carabobo, May 28, 1814
18. Second battle of La Puerta, June 15, 1814
19. Urica, December 5, 1814
20. Maturín, December 12, 1814
21. Bogotá, December 12, 1814
22. Cartegena, August 20–December 5, 1815
23. Cachiri, February 22, 1816
24. Cuchilla del Tambo, June 30, 1816
25. El Juncal, September 27, 1816
26. San Félix, April 11, 1817
27. Calabozo, February 12, 1818
28. Third battle of La Puerta, March 16, 1818
29. Ortiz, March 25, 1818
30. Rincón de los Toros, April 16, 1818
31. Cojedes, May 6, 1818
32. Las Queseras del Medio, April 3, 1819
33. Pantano de Vargas, July 25, 1819
34. Boyacá Bridge, August 7, 1819
35. Second battle of Carabobo, June 24, 1821
36. Yaguachi, August 19, 1821
37. Huaqui, September 12, 1821
38. Bombona, April 7, 1822
39. Pichincha, May 24, 1822
40. Lake Maracaibo, July 24, 1823
41. Tarqui, February 27, 1829

Retrato ecuestre de Bolívar, 1888, by Arturo
Michelena (1863–98). Bolívar was a wealthy
Creole who was deeply committed from a young
age to the cause of independence. His charisma
and perseverance carried him to leadership of
the Patriot armies in Venezuela and government
of Gran Colombia. (Palacio de Gobierno, Valencia,
Venezuela)

Pablo Morillo, c. 1815, by Pedro José Figueroa (1770–1838). Morillo rose through the ranks to become a general, an almost unimaginable feat in the Spanish Army. As commander of the largest expedition to the colonies, he oversaw the reconquest of Venezuela and New Granada. (Museo Nacional de Colombia)

Caracas, Bolívar ordered an evacuation: 20,000 civilians fled the city alongside Bolívar's troops.

By mid-August Bolívar reached Aragua, where he tried to assume command of all Patriot forces. The eastern generals refused to recognize him and both Bolívar and Mariño fled the country in disgrace. José Félix Ribas took over Bolívar's troops, while Francisco Bermúdez took Mariño's. Boves closed in with an army that had swelled to over 12,000, operating in several divisions. Boves relentlessly wore the Patriots down in a series of battles between September and November. The campaign culminated in the battle of Urica on December 5, 1814. The Patriot army was crushed, but not before Boves was killed leading a cavalry charge. Ribas was captured a few days after the battle and executed. Bermúdez escaped and spent the next three years leading a highly effective guerrilla resistance. Morales took command of the Llaneros, finishing the campaign with a victory

at Maturín on December 12, but the loss of Boves splintered Llanero loyalty, opening the door for a new leader and new alliances.

Nariño's capture reignited the civil war in New Granada. The exiled Bolívar arrived just in time to take command of the United Provinces army and lay siege to Bogotá. Bolívar defeated the Centralist troops on December 12, 1814 and Cundinamarca was absorbed into the United Provinces. Bolívar then marched against Royalist Santa Marta. Patriot Cartagena, fearing Bolívar's intentions, refused to aid his troops. Bolívar besieged the city. The two Patriot armies skirmished frequently from March 25 until May 8, when Bolívar unexpectedly resigned and went into voluntary exile in Jamaica.

About this time word reached Cartagena of the April arrival of a 12,000-man Spanish expedition under General Pablo Morillo. Quito was completely under Royalist control, while only scattered guerrilla groups remained in Venezuela. Only New Granada remained independent, leaving little doubt where Morillo intended to strike. After brief stops to subjugate Margarita Island and strengthen Royalist government in Caracas, Morillo sailed to Santa Marta. On August 20 he laid siege to Cartagena. Disease and starvation took a heavy toll on both sides, but the city fell on December 5, 1815, with only a handful of desperate Patriots slipping past the Spanish naval blockade to freedom.

Once Morillo gained Cartagena, he set about pacifying the rest of New Granada. Judging the Patriots too weak to oppose him, he divided his forces into columns in order to capture the country more quickly. The offensive began in early February, meeting only sporadic and ineffective opposition despite a brave Patriot stand at Cachiri on February 22, 1816. Bogotá fell on May 6. The last of the Patriot opposition was defeated at the battle of Cuchilla del Tambo, near Popayán, on June 30, 1816.

Bolívar returned to Venezuela after spending 1815 in exile in Jamaica and Haiti. He assembled a small fleet of eight schooners, four of which were privateers, and a few hundred followers. The fleet made for Margarita Island, which revolted almost as soon as Morillo left. The Patriots captured a Spanish brig and schooner on May 2, but as soon as they landed Mariño and Piar left the army. Bolívar, as always, had his sights on Caracas. Bolívar took 600 men and sailed to Ocumare on July 6. The campaign collapsed on July 9 after a single skirmish. Bolívar abandoned his troops and fled to Haiti. His army fought their way to Barcelona, where they met up with Piar. The combined Patriot army defeated the pursuing Royalists under Morales at the battle of El Juncal on September 27.

The most crucial development of 1816 was the rise of José Antonio Páez (1790–1873) as commander of the Llaneros. The Llaneros followed individual leaders rather than any particular political faction, and Páez, who was as personally brave as Boves, soon brought large numbers under the Patriot banner. Páez was a much better tactician and strategist than Boves, which immediately became apparent as he won a series of small battles against Royalists attempting to secure the plains. As Páez grew in strength, so did several other regional Caudillos. By the end of the year, much of southern and eastern Venezuela was in Patriot hands. All they needed was a base.

Bolívar returned to Venezuela on December 31, 1816. He realized the lack of a clear leader was crippling the Patriot cause. He set about making himself that leader by any means. Mariño resisted but Bolívar gained the support of Páez, Piar, and Bermúdez, who only a few months before had chased Bolívar down a beach, drawn sword in hand. Piar won an important victory at the battle of San Félix on April 11, 1817 that cut off the Royalist garrison at Angostura, a small port town on the Orinoco River. The starving Royalist garrison escaped by sailing downriver to open water. Harassed by the Patriot navy, they eventually reached the British island of Grenada. This defeat forced Morillo to terminate a campaign to retake Margarita and divert the troops to mainland garrisons. Margartia became an important Patriot naval base for protecting

the Orinoco basin. Bolívar formed a new government at Angostura and, with an open sea-lane, large stockpiles of surplus British arms and equipment began to arrive, along with the vanguard of over 6,000 British mercenaries. Bolívar strengthened his position by having Piar executed on controversial charges. Besides eliminating a potential rival, Bolívar had an eye on maintaining control over his troops. While in Haiti, he had promised to free all slaves in return for assistance. Executing the popular Mulatto assured the members of the white power structure that they remained firmly in control. Piar's execution also brought Mariño into the fold. The Patriots were unified.

With a unified command and a secure base of operations, Bolívar set about planning his next campaign. Unsurprisingly, the goal was Caracas. Bolívar united forces from eastern Venezuela with Páez's Llaneros. Together they marched on Morillo, who was in Calabozo. They defeated the Royalists on February 12, 1818 but Morillo escaped with a large portion of his army. Bolívar demanded a march north to Caracas, but Páez refused to take his troops out of the plains. Bolívar split his army and marched without Páez. Morillo called in reinforcements, most notably Morales, who commanded a large Royalist division. Bolívar tried to escape the trap but was too late. He made a stand at the third battle of La Puerta on March 16, 1818. Just as Morales' division began to give way, Morillo appeared, leading the decisive charge. Bolívar's army was shattered. Morillo was severely wounded and had to relinquish command for the remainder of the campaign. Bolívar retreated to reunite with Páez. On April 16, he was surprised at Rincón de los Toros by a group of Royalist cavalry. The Royalist commander sent a small party to infiltrate the Patriot camp and nearly succeeded in killing Bolívar. At dawn the Royalists launched a full attack, and the fleeing Bolívar was forced to throw away his uniform to avoid recognition. Páez fared little better, being defeated by a Royalist division at Cojedes on May 6. Morales recaptured Calabozo on May 20, 1818.

A map of the third battle of La Puerta (March 16, 1818), no date. Although the armies were much smaller in Spanish America, the style of fighting was very similar to that of the Peninsular War. Armies used the same tactics and formations as found in Europe. (Biblioteca Nacional de España; photograph by author)

Bolívar spent the remainder of 1818 rebuilding his shattered army and maintaining control over his commanders. Páez toyed with the idea of overthrowing Bolívar, but quickly abandoned the idea. The two Patriot armies reunited, and in March Bolívar arrived from a trip to Angostura accompanied by a battalion of British infantry. In 1817 Bolívar's agents began recruiting men in Britain and Ireland. The first arrived in late 1817, and after the 1818 campaign small units of British infantry, artillery, and cavalry appeared in the Patriot ranks. Shipments of men continued to arrive through November 1819. Over 6,000 men, some of them veterans of Wellington's army, signed up for the Patriot cause. Most died or deserted before ever seeing combat, but enough remained to field several battalions of skilled, confident soldiers. The arrival of these troops boosted Patriot morale and training and caused great concern among the Spanish officers, many of whom had served alongside the British during the Peninsular campaign.

Morillo reassumed command of the Royalist army and began an offensive in February 1819. Bolívar had no wish to repeat the disaster of 1818 and avoided battle, allowing Páez to draw the Royalists deep into the Llanos plains, where attrition due to hunger, exposure, and disease devastated the Royalists more surely than Patriot arms. Páez won an important local victory at Las Queseras del Medio on April 3. The armies were deployed for battle near the Araure River, and Páez, with 150 Llaneros, cleverly baited the Royalist cavalry by exhausting their horses. When the Royalist cavalry was blown, he suddenly turned and charged, defeating over 1,000 of the enemy. Without his cavalry Morillo declined battle and ended the campaign.

At this point Bolívar unveiled a new plan. For once he forsook Caracas. Páez would keep the Royalists occupied on the plains while Bolívar took a division and marched on Bogotá. It was a rash, almost reckless plan that involved marching across hundreds of miles of plains in the torrential rainy season and then crossing the Andes, despite lacking uniforms and supplies. As Bolívar reached the Andes, he was joined by a Colombian division under Francisco de Paula Santander (1792–1840). The Patriots suffered terribly during the crossing, but the move took the Royalists completely by surprise. Nevertheless, Bolívar was nearly destroyed at the battle of Pantano de Vargas on July 25,

his army only saved by the tenacious fighting of 150 British volunteers and a heroic charge by 14 Llanero cavalry under Juan José Rondón. He recovered and inflicted a complete defeat on the Royalists at Boyacá

Vuelvan Caras (detail), 1890, by Arturo Michelena (1863–98). Llanero cavalry in battle. The figure in the foreground has a blood-soaked lance from a previous victim while his compatriot displays a "War to the Death" pennant, indicating that prisoners should expect no mercy. (Colección del círculo militar, Venezuela)

Batalla de Boyacá (detail), 1890, by Martín Tovar y Tovar (1827–1902). One area where warfare differed from Europe was the frequency of hand-to-hand combat. Troops commonly crossed swords and bayonets, and factors like historical rivalries, codes of honor, and War to the Death only exacerbated the ferocity of the fighting. (Palacio Federal Legislativo, Venezuela)

Bridge on August 7. Bolívar occupied Bogotá on August 11. He formed a new government with Santander as vice president. On September 11, Bolívar began the long journey back to Angostura. When he arrived on December 11 there were several days of celebration. Bolívar then convened Congress to present a grand vision for the newly liberated territories. Rather than return to the colonial division of New Granada and Venezuela, they would merge. The country of Gran Colombia was born.

For several years, Spain had been assembling another major expedition at Cádiz. At dawn on January 1, 1820 Colonel Rafael del Riego, a regimental commander, assembled his troops on their parade ground

and declared, "Long live the Constitution of 1812." His act of defiance sparked a full rebellion by the army. Although he was unable to take the city, Riego sent troops into the countryside. The rebellion spread quickly, as Ferdinand VII's remaining troops had no stomach for civil war. On July 9 the entire royal family swore loyalty to the newly reinstalled Cortes. The Cortes reinstated the 1812 Constitution and sent word to America to negotiate with the Patriots "as brothers."

Morillo downplayed the news as it arrived in Venezuela, fearing its effect on the army and populace, but word quickly spread. Although he immediately complied with orders, proclaiming the Constitution on June 7 and opening negotiations with Bolívar, the Riego revolt crushed Morillo's spirit. Since 1818 he had written increasingly pessimistic reports that without reinforcements he could not maintain control of the country, much less put down the rebellion. Without hope of reinforcement, he requested to be relieved

Batalla de Boyacá, no date, artist unknown. This period illustration shows the chaos of battle but also illustrates the ability of commanders to survey the entire field, a luxury usually not available to European commanders due to the much larger size of the armies in European warfare. (Casa Museo Quinta de Bolívar, Colombia; photograph by René Chartrand)

of command. On November 26 a six-month armistice was ratified. Morillo and Bolívar met the next day to signal its implementation. On December 17, 1820 Pablo Morillo sailed for Spain, leaving command to Miguel de La Torre, one of his divisional commanders.

At the end of January 1821, Urdaneta, commanding a Patriot division near the Royalist town of Maracaibo, engineered a takeover of the city. La Torre declared this a breach of the armistice and notified Bolívar hostilities would resume on April 28. Bolívar immediately began planning for another drive on Caracas. He ordered Páez and Urdaneta to rendezvous with his division at San Carlos for a drive on the capital. Bermúdez would create a diversion by striking from the east. As in 1813, the Royalists had more troops than the Patriots, but Bolívar had the initiative and a clear goal. Bermúdez made excellent progress, actually reaching Caracas before Bolívar. The Royalists responded by sending Morales with their best division against Bermudez. Meanwhile, the main Patriot army

concentrated on June 7. Belatedly, La Torre recalled Morales. The two armies met on June 24, 1821 on the same field where Bolívar won his great victory at Carabobo in 1814. Bolívar had 6,500 men, La Torre just over 4,000. A charge by the British Legion battalion cracked the Royalist line, at which point Páez's Llaneros swept in and broke the army. Despite having several other columns nearby, one of which had routed Bermúdez at Caracas the day before, La Torre retreated to the safety of Puerto Cabello. Bolívar entered Caracas on June 28.

Prior to the Carabobo campaign, Bolívar had sent General Antonio José de Sucre to take command of a division operating in southern Colombia. In October 1820 the port of Guayaquil, in the captaincy general of Quito, had rebelled. Sucre's orders were to take his division to their aid. He sailed into Guayaquil and began a campaign towards Quito in mid-August. After an initial victory at Yaguachi on August 19, he was routed by Aymerich at Huaqui on September 12. Aymerich failed to pursue and Sucre spent the rest of the year building a new army.

As 1821 drew to a close, Bolívar began planning a pincer campaign against Quito – Bolívar from the north, Sucre from the south. Bolívar lost a third of his troops in a grueling march from Bogotá to Pasto. Arrogant after two years of victory, he

Batalla de Carabobo (detail), 1887, by Martín Tovar y Tovar (1827–1902). This section of Tovar y Tovar's sweeping masterpiece shows Páez's Llaneros surging past fallen Patriot infantry in the second battle of Carabobo, 1821. The black soldier in the foreground is Pedro Camejo, also known as "Primero Negro." An ex-slave renowned for his bravery, Camejo was mortally wounded during the battle. (Palacio Federal Legislativo, Venezuela)

charged across a ravine at a dug-in Royalist position at Bombona, west of Pasto, on April 7, 1822. His men were slaughtered. Luckily the British-officered Rifles battalion outflanked the Royalists, forcing them from their positions. Bolívar won the field but lost 40 percent of his army. The Royalists withdrew intact.

With only 1,800 men, Sucre realized he did not have the forces necessary for an offensive and asked General José de San Martín, campaigning in Peru since 1820, for assistance. San Martín sent a 1,200-man Peruvian division. Sucre met the Peruvians at Saraguro in early February 1822. He executed a careful advance north, shadowed by Royalist cavalry. The threat of a sudden raid was so severe he assigned the half-British Albion battalion, the best infantry in his army, to guard the baggage train. Finally reaching Quito on May 23, he saw Aymerich's 2,000 Royalists entrenched in a strong defensive position. Sucre tried to bypass them by climbing Pichincha volcano, immediately west of the city, but was caught in a rainstorm and spotted at dawn on May 24. Aymerich quickly doubled back and fought a brutal slugging match on the slopes of the volcano, which was only decided when the Albion battalion defeated a Spanish battalion that was on the verge of flanking the Patriot line. The Royalists retreated into the city. Aymerich surrendered the next day.

Río de la Plata

When the Buenos Aires junta deposed Viceroy Cisneros on May 25, 1810, they assumed leadership over all of Río de la Plata, an assumption that immediately led to conflict with Royalists and tension with other Patriot provinces in the viceroyalty. The junta's first move was to bring Upper Peru back under its control. A 1,200-man expedition left Buenos Aires on July 9, 1810. Antonio González Balcarce commanded the troops while a political commissioner, Juan José Castelli, was placed in charge of civilian matters. The first stop was Córdoba, where Liniers, who had been organizing Royalist opposition, was captured and executed. The army continued through Salta, Tucumán, and Jujuy, confirming the support of each region. Crossing into Upper Peru, they were defeated by a Royalist column at the battle of Cotagaita on October 29, 1810, but defeated the pursuing Royalists at Suipacha on November 7.

Another expedition of 950 men under Manuel Belgrano (1770–1820) was outfitted to march into Paraguay. Paraguayans, long resentful of Buenos Aires' economic domination, responded to the new junta by convening their own open council. They decided to remain loyal to Spain but maintain friendly relations with Buenos Aires – in effect, to stay neutral. Buenos Aires

viewed this as defiance. The Patriots left Buenos Aires in late October 1810 and advanced up the Paraguay River towards Asunción, the capital. Expecting little opposition, Belgrano soon faced an army of 5,000 poorly armed but fanatical Paraguayan peasants. Belgrano was defeated in two hard-fought battles at Paraguarí (January 19) and Tacuarí (March 9). He negotiated a truce and withdrew. The Paraguayans, flushed with victory earned without Spanish aid, deposed the Spanish governor and declared independence on May 17, 1811. The country became consumed by internal politics and was not involved in any other military action during the wars of independence.

In Montevideo, capital of the province of Banda Oriental, Royalist governor Francisco Javier de Elío began planning a campaign against Buenos Aires. His first step was to defeat the Patriots in his own province. He dispatched 1,200 men against 1,100 Patriots concentrating north of the city under the leadership of José Gervasio Artigas (1764–1850), a long-time frontier cavalry officer. The Royalists were defeated at the battle of Las Piedras on May 18, 1811. Artigas, joining forces with a division from Buenos Aires led by José Rondeau, besieged Montevideo. The Patriots lacked the heavy artillery needed to breach the city walls while the Royalists defeated a small Patriot fleet, enabling them to keep the harbor open for supplies. Trapped in a stalemate, Elío asked for Portuguese assistance. There was a long history of conflict between Spain and Portugal over the Banda Oriental and the Portuguese monarch, John VI, wasted no time in seizing the opportunity. In July 4,000 Brazilian Portuguese troops marched into the Banda Oriental, forcing the Patriots to break the siege. It soon became apparent the Portuguese did not intend to leave. Panicked, Elío concluded a truce with Buenos Aires on October 20. Artigas was excluded and forced to retreat, along with thousands of civilians, to the neighboring province of Entre Ríos. Henceforth Artigas became convinced of the need to earn

Battles and sieges in Río de la Plata and the surrounding region

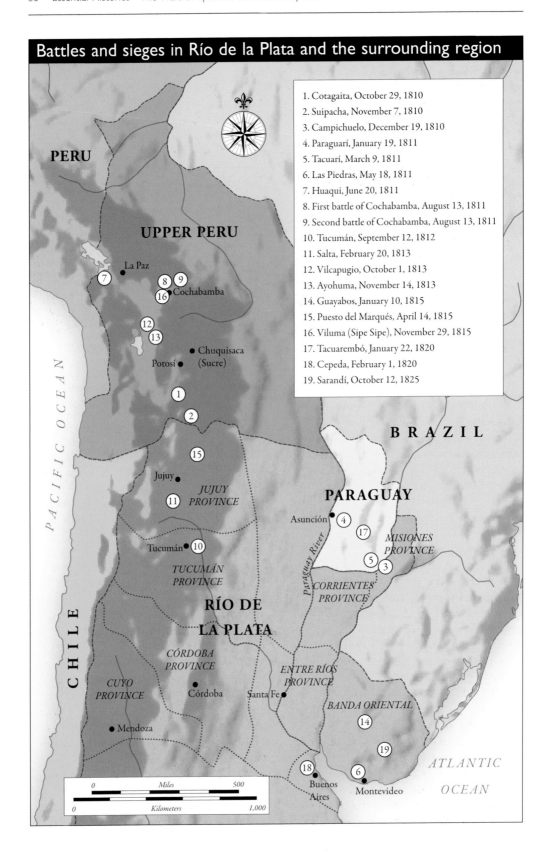

1. Cotagaita, October 29, 1810
2. Suipacha, November 7, 1810
3. Campichuelo, December 19, 1810
4. Paraguarí, January 19, 1811
5. Tacuarí, March 9, 1811
6. Las Piedras, May 18, 1811
7. Huaqui, June 20, 1811
8. First battle of Cochabamba, August 13, 1811
9. Second battle of Cochabamba, August 13, 1811
10. Tucumán, September 12, 1812
11. Salta, February 20, 1813
12. Vilcapugio, October 1, 1813
13. Ayohuma, November 14, 1813
14. Guayabos, January 10, 1815
15. Puesto del Marqués, April 14, 1815
16. Viluma (Sipe Sipe), November 29, 1815
17. Tacuarembó, January 22, 1820
18. Cepeda, February 1, 1820
19. Sarandí, October 12, 1825

PERU

UPPER PERU

La Paz

Cochabamba

Chuquisaca
(Sucre)

Potosí

PACIFIC OCEAN

BRAZIL

Jujuy

JUJUY
PROVINCE

PARAGUAY

Asunción

MISIONES
PROVINCE

Tucumán

Paraguay River

CORRIENTES
PROVINCE

TUCUMÁN
PROVINCE

RÍO DE
LA PLATA

CÓRDOBA
PROVINCE

ENTRE RÍOS
PROVINCE

CHILE

CUYO
PROVINCE

Córdoba

Santa Fe

BANDA ORIENTAL

Mendoza

ATLANTIC
OCEAN

0   Miles   500

Buenos
Aires

Montevideo

0   Kilometers   1,000

independence from all outside powers –
Spain, Portugal, and Buenos Aires.

After their victory at Suipacha, the
Patriots had advanced through Upper
Peru to the Peruvian border. There, Castelli
signed a 40-day truce with the Royalist
commander, Jose Manuel Goyeneche. On
June 20, 1811, a few days before the truce
expired, Goyeneche attacked the Patriots
at Huaqui. The Royalists won a crushing
victory, causing the Patriots to withdraw
completely from Upper Peru. The defeat
caused the collapse of the junta and Castelli
and Balcarce were both relieved by the new
government, which was called the First
Triumvirate since executive power was held
by a three man council. Goyeneche spent
the next year pacifying Upper Peru and
dealing with an Indian rebellion in Peru.
He won two major battles at Cochabamba
against poorly trained local troops, one on
August 13, 1811 and the other on May 27,
1812. On September 3, 1812 the Royalists
finally sent a division under Pío de Tristán
into Río de la Plata. Tristán was defeated by
Belgrano, who had been assigned Patriot
command, at Tucumán on September 12.

Tucumán signaled a turn in Patriot
fortunes. The First Triumvirate collapsed in
October and was replaced by a more radical

Fortaleza General Artigas. This fort, commissioned
by Francisco Javier de Elío, was not completed until after
the wars. Such fortresses were common defenses at
colonial ports and were nearly impregnable against
besieging forces that typically lacked heavy artillery.
(Departamento de Estudios Históricos del Estado
Mayor del Ejército, Uruguay)

Second Triumvirate. On January 31, 1813 the
Second Triumvirate summoned an assembly
to write a new constitution and adopt other
symbols of a new republic, even though it
did not declare total independence. Belgrano
spent the remainder of 1812 building his
strength, and in early 1813 launched a new
offensive into Upper Peru. He destroyed
Tristán's division at Salta on February 20,
1813 and slowly continued north. Fresh
Patriot forces formed throughout Upper
Peru, most notably in Cochabamba, and
Royalist fortunes hit a low ebb. In October
Joaquín de la Pezuela replaced Goyeneche.
Pezuela quickly reorganized his forces and
restored morale. The rejuvenated Royalists
forced Belgrano into battle at Vilcapugio on
October 1, 1813. In one of the most evenly
balanced battles of the war, the Royalists
outlasted the Patriots as a single late-arriving
Royalist cavalry squadron decided the day.
Pezuela defeated the Patriots again at
Ayohuma on November 14. The remnants

La Hércules persiguiendo a Mercurio frente a Montevideo, c. 1890, by Eduardo de Martino (1838–1912). In May 1814 a Río de la Plata fleet under William Brown defeated a Spanish fleet protecting Montevideo, forcing the Royalist garrison's surrender. Here the Patriot flagship, *Hércules,* chases the Spanish frigate *Mercurio* back into the harbor. (Estado Mayor General de la Armada, Argentina)

of Belgrano's shattered army limped back to Jujuy, where they found the Second Triumvirate had been replaced by yet another new government headed by a single Supreme Director.

Even as his offensive failed, Belgrano detached two officers, Ignacio Warnes and Juan Antonio Álvarez de Arenales, to recruit troops in eastern Upper Peru. Several local Caudillos organized their own bands and soon eight "Republiquetas," or small republics, were created. Each was a territory where a specific guerrilla band operated. These guerrilla forces differed from others in the wars as they often engaged in set-piece combats using regular formations and tactics. From 1814 until 1817, numerous small, vicious campaigns were fought in eastern and southern Upper Peru as the Royalists methodically eliminated the Republiquetas one at a time. Nevertheless, the Republiquetas provided an important contribution to the struggle as local citizens fought for their own independence instead of relying on Buenos Aires.

In the Banda Oriental, British diplomatic pressure led to Portuguese withdrawal in 1812. Rondeau and Artigas immediately returned and reinstated the siege of Montevideo on October 20. As in the previous year, the Patriots did not have the land strength to storm the walls or the navy to blockade the harbor. Lacking shipbuilding facilities, Buenos Aires purchased ships and crews in late 1813 through an agent in the United States. Crewed mostly by British, Irish, and American sailors, the new fleet was commanded by William Brown, an Irish American who had served in the British Royal Navy. Brown executed a methodical campaign down the Río de la Plata in 1814, winning naval battles on March 15 and May 17 that finally sealed off Montevideo. Realizing the situation was now hopeless, the Royalists surrendered on June 23, 1814. Artigas formed the provinces of Banda Oriental, Corrientes, Santa Fe, Misiones, Entre Ríos, and Córdoba into a confederation called the Federal League, designed to counter the dominance of Centralist Buenos Aires; the two sides soon fell into conflict and Federal League troops defeated a small Buenos Aires force at Guayabos on January 10, 1815.

Despite tension with the Federal League, Buenos Aires used the fall of Montevideo to plan another expedition to Upper Peru. Rondeau was given command, accompanied by most of the forces that had been part of the siege. Rondeau launched his offensive in January 1815 but some of his commanders revolted, claiming it was not specifically ordered by Buenos Aires. Rondeau overcame the opposition, but conflict between Patriot commanders became a hallmark of the campaign. The Patriots won a combat at Puesto del Marqués on April 14, but lost the services of Martín Miguel de Güemes (1785–1821), a brave and tenacious officer who had first made his name during the British invasion of 1807, who fell out with Rondeau and returned to Salta with 300 Gaucho cavalry. Rondeau took Potosí in mid-May and then stopped his advance. It was a fatal pause. At the beginning of the campaign, the Royalists could only field 2,500 men as most of their forces were fighting another Indian rebellion that had erupted around Cuzco in 1814. By the time Rondeau took to the field again in October, Pezuela had concentrated a veteran army of over 5,000 men, including several hundred Spanish regulars. Rondeau had 3,500 lesser-quality troops. The result was predictable. Pezuela easily defeated the Patriots at Viluma (a.k.a. Sipe Sipe), just outside Cochabamba, on November 29, 1815.

Even as they fought the Republiquetas, the Royalists focused on their overall strategy of reconquering Río de la Plata. Between 1814 and 1821, the Royalists launched eight different expeditions with the goal of taking Jujuy, Salta, and Tucumán as a prerequisite for a drive on Buenos Aires. In these campaigns they were not met by the regular army. Instead, they were opposed by Gauchos, regional cowboys who worked the cattle ranches of the region. Gathered in regional bands that were loyal to a Caudillo, overall command of the Gaucho forces fell to Güemes. Gauchos fought a war of outposts,

hitting Royalist garrisons, foraging detachments and stragglers, but avoiding large, pitched battles. These were bitter campaigns of attrition, each of which ended in Royalist defeat. However, the Royalists became ever more skilled in this style of warfare. They repeatedly occupied Jujuy and Salta and forced Buenos Aires to maintain a regular army in the region at the expense of forces elsewhere. These campaigns also compelled Buenos Aires to give greater recognition to the provinces. When full independence was declared in 1816, it was by a Congress convened in Tucumán, not Buenos Aires. During the final campaign in 1821 the Royalists killed Güemes, but by then events had moved beyond a simple Patriot versus Royalist struggle. Buenos Aires, the United Provinces and the Federal League became embroiled in a civil war that lasted into the 1860s.

Peru

While Peru remained solidly Royalist, the Captaincy General of Chile did not. Far more self-sufficient and economically detached from Spain than Peru, Chile had been an autonomous region since 1778. It must have surprised few in Lima when Santiago formed a junta in September 1810. After a series of political upheavals that nearly plunged the province into civil war, the new Patriot government came under the dictatorial control of José Miguel Carrera (1785–1821), a newly returned veteran of the Peninsular campaign from a well-established aristocratic family.

In early 1813 Viceroy Abascal sent Colonel Antonio Pareja to Chile with a group of officers and stores of supplies to organize Royalist resistance. The southern frontier had remained Royalist and Pareja quickly raised 6,000 men. Carrera had 5,000, half armed with lances. The ensuing campaign was an embarrassment for both sides. The Royalist army deserted en masse and Pareja became ill and died. Carrera proved totally incompetent, repeatedly

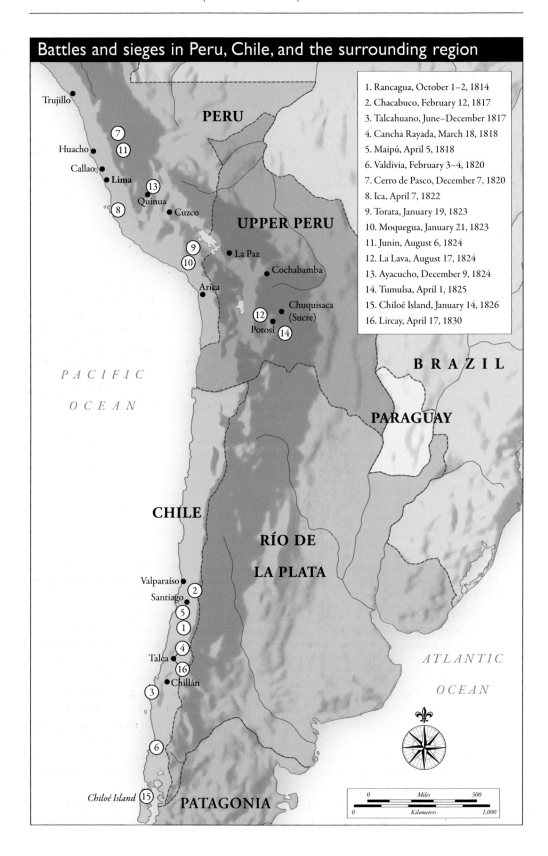

Battles and sieges in Peru, Chile, and the surrounding region

1. Rancagua, October 1–2, 1814
2. Chacabuco, February 12, 1817
3. Talcahuano, June–December 1817
4. Cancha Rayada, March 18, 1818
5. Maipú, April 5, 1818
6. Valdivia, February 3–4, 1820
7. Cerro de Pasco, December 7, 1820
8. Ica, April 7, 1822
9. Torata, January 19, 1823
10. Moquegua, January 21, 1823
11. Junin, August 6, 1824
12. La Lava, August 17, 1824
13. Ayacucho, December 9, 1824
14. Tumulsa, April 1, 1825
15. Chiloé Island, January 14, 1826
16. Lircay, April 17, 1830

defeated by a frontier captain leading the few hundred remaining Royalist troops. Carrera was deposed by his own officials who placed his rival, Bernardo O'Higgins (1778–1842), in command. O'Higgins fought the reorganized and reinforced Royalists to a standstill in the early months of 1814, but then negotiated a treaty that caused outrage on both sides. A barracks mutiny in Santiago returned Carrera to power and resulted in a brief civil war. The conflict quickly subsided on news that a 5,000-man Royalist army under Mariano Osorio had gathered at Talcahuano. Carrera and O'Higgins joined forces, but lost to the Royalists at Rancagua on October 1–2, 1814 when Carrera refused to march to O'Higgins' assistance. Osorio entered Santiago on October 9 as Patriot troops and officials fled across the Andes to the town of Mendoza.

In September 1814 Colonel José de San Martín arrived in Mendoza as governor of Cuyo province. San Martín was a Creole who had joined the Spanish army in 1790 at the age of 12. He first saw combat against the

Últimos Momentos en Rancagua, 1944, by Pedro Subercaseaux (1880–1956). Surrounded and nearly out of ammunition, Chilean general Bernardo O'Higgins prepares to lead a desperate charge through the Royalist lines at Rancagua in 1814. Numerous battles were fought in the central plazas of colonial towns. (Comandancia en Jefe del Ejército, Chile)

Moors in Oran in 1791. He fought the French in 1793–94, at Bailén in 1808, and at Albuera in 1811. He served in both line and light infantry and as a commander of cavalry, a general's aide, and a training instructor. He retired in August 1811 and, after a visit to London where he was introduced in Patriot circles, returned to Buenos Aires in early 1812. He showcased his talents by raising a regiment of horse grenadiers whose training and discipline far surpassed anything previously seen in Patriot service.

San Martín proposed a grand strategy for winning the war. Peru had to be defeated. Geography guaranteed an attack through Upper Peru would never succeed. The only route was a flanking attack by sea, through

Chile. San Martín would raise an army of 4,000–4,500 men, liberate Chile, and from there take Peru. The government approved the plan. He was promoted to brigadier general and set about building the Army of the Andes. Over the next two years, Cuyo was set on a war economy with rations, forced loans, and compulsory labor. Troops were meticulously trained and supplied with officers schooled in the latest tactics. Logistical and support elements, often secondary considerations in Patriot armies, were developed, and a spy network implemented throughout Chile. The army proved its quality in a flawless 18-day crossing of the Andes, followed by its complete defeat of a Royalist division at Chacabuco on February 12, 1817.

Paso de los Andes, 1948, by Frans van Riel (1879–1950). Here, San Martín oversees his well-supplied and orderly troops as they execute their daring march across the rugged Andes. (Museo Granaderos a Caballo General San Martín, Argentina)

The Royalists hastily abandoned Santiago for their bases in the south.

Upon entering Santiago, San Martín organized a Chilean government headed by O'Higgins. He returned to Buenos Aires to seek resources for the next stage of his plan, leaving O'Higgins to mop up the Royalist forces. Unknown to either, a skilled and charismatic Spanish colonel, José Ordóñez, had taken command of the Royalist forces, concentrated at the strategically important port of Talcahuano. Ordóñez withstood a six-month Patriot siege that ended in a disastrous assault on December 6, 1817. O'Higgins was forced to raise the siege as Osorio arrived by sea at the head of a Royalist relief force. Combined with Ordóñez's men, the Royalists now had about 5,000 troops.

San Martín, who had returned in May 1817, assumed the role of supreme commander. He gathered a division of troops and united with O'Higgins. Together the Patriots had about 8,000 men. Osorio had

Details from *Batalla de Maipú*, 1954, by Pedro Subercaseaux (1880–1956). He captures the mood of the last years of the war: attacking Patriots surging towards unstoppable victory, defending Royalists alternately grimly fighting to the last or surrendering to the inevitable. (Museo Histórico del Carmen, Chile; photograph by Marco Benevente)

The battle of Maipú, April 5, 1818

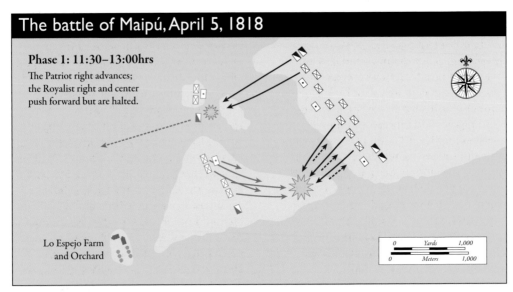

Phase 1: 11:30–13:00hrs

The Patriot right advances;
the Royalist right and center
push forward but are halted.

Lo Espejo Farm
and Orchard

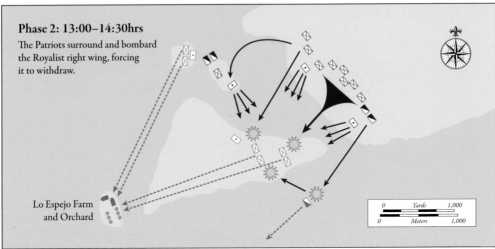

Phase 2: 13:00–14:30hrs

The Patriots surround and bombard
the Royalist right wing, forcing
it to withdraw.

Lo Espejo Farm
and Orchard

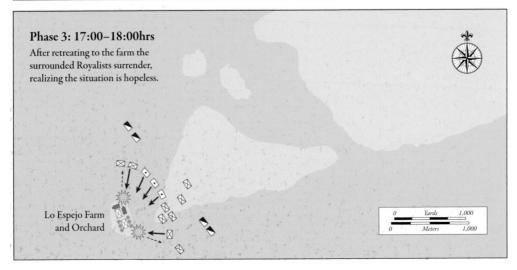

Phase 3: 17:00–18:00hrs

After retreating to the farm the
surrounded Royalists surrender,
realizing the situation is hopeless.

Lo Espejo Farm
and Orchard

launched an offensive northward, but when he saw the size of the army against him he attempted to retreat back to Talcahuano. San Martín caught up with him at Cancha Rayada on March 18, 1818. Trapped with his back to a river, Osorio lost his nerve. Ordóñez assumed command and launched a bold night-time attack, routing O'Higgins' division and seriously wounding O'Higgins. The other Patriot division withdrew intact. It was a serious defeat, but Osorio dithered and San Martín rallied his army. When they met again at Maipú on April 5, San Martín had 5,500 men to Osorio's 4,500. The Patriots dispersed the Royalists in a hard-fought battle. Although fighting continued in Chile until 1826, independence was secured.

After the victory at Maipú, San Martín set about the final phase of his campaign, the liberation of Peru. However, support dried up as the new Chilean government focused on cementing its own independence, while Río de la Plata descended into conflict with the Federal League. Events came to a head when Buenos Aires ordered San Martín to return

with the army to fight in the civil war. San Martín ignored the order. Without hope of reserves, San Martín gathered his army, which he called the United Army. In August 1820, 4,500 men sailed for Lima, protected by a new Chilean squadron under Thomas Cochrane. The Royalists had over 14,000 men in Peru and another 9,000 in Upper Peru. Aware that losing a single battle would doom the entire project, San Martín adhered to a strict strategy of allowing Peruvians to liberate themselves. After landing in Peru on September 11, 1820, he detached a flying column to encourage the provinces to rise up while he sought out a base of operations, ending the year in Huacho, a suitable port town adjacent to a fertile valley. Cochrane scored a major victory by capturing the

El abrazo de Maipú, 1908, by Pedro Subercaseaux (1880–1956). During the battle of Maipú, Bernardo O'Higgins was recuperating from a serious wound in nearby Santiago. Gathering the town's militia, cadets and invalid troops, he rushed to the sound of battle. Upon seeing the Patriot victory he tearfully embraced San Martín. (Museo Histórico Nacional, Argentina)

Vista de la ciudad de Mendoza, 1860, by P. Mousse.
Mendoza was a quiet town in a newly created province
at the foot of the Andes when José de San Martín
became governor in 1814. Over the next two years he
completely transformed the town, putting it on a total
war footing. (Instituto Nacional Sanmartiniano, Argentina)

largest remaining Spanish ship in the Pacific,
a 44-gun frigate, while the flying column
won a victory at Cerro de Pasco on
December 7.

San Martín received more good news at
the beginning of 1821 as most of northern
Peru declared for the Patriots. San Martín
was acclaimed "The Protector" and placed
in charge of liberated Peru. On January 21
the Royalist army deposed Viceroy Pezuela
and replaced him with José de La Serna, a
Liberal Spanish general. San Martín entered
negotiations with the Royalists while sending
two more flying columns to inspire the south
to rise. Meanwhile, both sides were being
ravaged by diseases common in Peru's coastal
climate. On July 6 La Serna abandoned Lima,
but maintained a garrison in the critical
nearby port fortress of Callao. It was exactly
what San Martín had hoped for – to take the
capital without a fight. He occupied Lima,
but found no enthusiasm for independence.

After negotiations collapsed, the Royalists
undermined San Martín by marching an
army to evacuate the garrison at Callao,
deliberately presenting their flank to the
deployed Patriots. San Martín refused to
take the bait, enraging his officers. It was
a fatal decision that cost San Martín the
confidence of his army. The impetuous
Cochrane, disgusted with San Martín's
strategy and his sailors' lack of pay, seized
the Patriot treasury and sailed off to patrol
the Pacific independently. He resigned from
Chilean service in November 1822; in 1823
he was named admiral of the newly
independent Brazilian navy.

Still unwilling to risk his own forces, San
Martín opened the year by committing the
new Peruvian army to battle. A division was
sent to aide Sucre in Quito while another
division was sent to Ica, which had declared
for the Patriots. The Royalists destroyed
the Patriots at Ica on April 7, 1822, but
the other division helped liberate Quito.
With the Patriots of the north and south
now in direct contact San Martín and
Bolívar met in Guayaquil on July 26–27
to settle outstanding political and strategic
questions. Their meeting was private and
the discussions have been the source of

controversy ever since. A middle-ground interpretation is that San Martín came seeking troops for Peru while Bolívar planned to eliminate a rival. If true, both men achieved their aim. San Martín returned to Lima, formed a civilian government, and resigned command on September 20, 1822. He then departed into self-imposed exile in France. But Bolívar, and the full weight of his army, was now committed to Peru.

Despite San Martín's resignation, the army tried to execute his final proposals. Having gained Lima and believing Bolívar would soon arrive, San Martín thought the time was finally ripe to strike. Rudecindo Alvarado, who had taken command of the United Army, launched a campaign in December 1822, landing in Arica. Jerónimo Valdés (1784–1855) and José de Canterac (1787–1835) rushed south to intercept him. Valdés defeated Alvarado at Torata on January 19, 1823. Canterac arrived at the end of the battle and the combined Royalist forces completed the destruction of the Patriot army two days later at Moquegua.

When word arrived of the Patriot defeat, the Peruvian government fell into anarchy. Andrés de Santa Cruz, the commander of the Peruvian army, demanded Congress replace the three-man junta that acted as the executive with a single new president, José Bernardo de Tagle, Marquis of Torre Tagle. Congress deposed the junta but instead elected José de la Riva Agüero, an aristocrat from Lima, president. Santa Cruz, who had commanded the Peruvian division under Sucre and gained the favor of Bolívar, immediately wrote to "The Liberator" for help. Bolívar sent a division of 3,000 Colombian troops. Riva Agüero fled to Trujillo, where he established a rival government while Torre Tagle took charge in Lima.

Believing the matter settled, Santa Cruz assembled 6,500 men for another expedition, driving deep into Upper Peru before panicking in September in the face of a united Royalist army. His subsequent retreat cost over 2,000 men. On September 1 Bolívar arrived in Callao. Riva Agüero responded by raising 3,000 troops and trying to negotiate a temporary alliance with the Royalists to

drive all foreigners out of Peru. Fortunately for Bolívar, one of Riva Agüero's officers arrested him on November 25. Bolívar had him sent into exile.

With government restored, Bolívar set about consolidating control, gathering Colombian reinforcements, and rebuilding the Peruvian army. Preparations were disrupted when the garrison of Callao, which consisted of the forgotten remnants of San Martín's army, rebelled in February 1824. Initially demanding nothing more than back pay, they eventually raised the Spanish flag. A Royalist division soon occupied Lima but Bolívar was unfazed, well aware the Royalists faced a rebellion of their own. Pedro Antonio Olañeta, a merchant from Salta who had risen through the Royalist ranks to become one of their most effective generals, commanded all troops in Upper Peru. Olañeta had learned of Ferdinand's second restoration in late 1823. A staunch Absolutist, Olañeta feared that La Serna, a well-known Constitutionalist, would defect on hearing the news, so he simply beat him to the punch, declaring La Serna a Liberal traitor. La Serna was forced to detach Valdés with 7,000 men to deal with Olañeta.

Meanwhile, Bolívar concentrated his forces for the final campaign. By the end of July his army was gathered at Cerro de Pasco. La Serna sent Canterac with 8,000 men against him. The armies met on a marshy plain at Junin on August 6, 1824. In a scene reminiscent of the Middle Ages, the infantry on both sides watched as the cavalry fought the battle. Despite being outnumbered and nearly routed, the Patriot cavalry recovered and won the day. Although he only lost 250 men, Canterac was stunned. He feared he would be cut off in hostile territory and began a precipitate retreat to Cuzco, 450 miles to the south.

Desperate, La Serna recalled the division from Lima as well as Valdés' forces. Valdés and Olañeta had fought an indecisive battle at La Lava, near Potosí, on August 17. They concluded a hasty truce and Valdés raced back via forced marches. On 6 October Bolívar relinquished command to Sucre.

Batalla de Ayacucho, c. 1890, by Martín Tovar y Tovar (1827–1902). The last major battle in Spanish America was also one of the most epic. Outnumbered and desperate, a Patriot army that contained troops from Peru, Gran Colombia, Chile, and Río de la Plata won a crushing victory that finally broke the Royalists' will. (Galería de Arte Nacional, Venezuela)

It was an odd decision for a man convinced of his own greatness on the cusp of closing his final glorious campaign. Historians have cited plans to besiege Callao, bring a new Colombian division to the front, or deal with political upheaval in Bogotá, but these excuses ring hollow. The first two are not tasks for a commander-in-chief and Lima was too distant to affect events in Bogotá. More likely, Bolívar simply feared defeat.

Sucre faced a difficult situation. Nearly at the gates of Cuzco, he found the hunter had become the hunted. With the arrival of his recalled divisions La Serna had over 9,300 men, while the Patriot army had dwindled to about 6,000. Outnumbered and far from his base, in late October Sucre decided to withdraw. The two armies spent all of November in a cat-and-mouse series of marches trying to gain advantage. La Serna nearly caught Sucre in a trap on December 3, but a valiant rear-guard action fought by the Rifles battalion saved the day. Despite losing over half their men, they stalled the Royalists long enough for Sucre to escape. Their sacrifice paid a handsome reward on December 9 on a mesa near the town of Quinua. With the Royalists encamped on a hill above him, Sucre made his stand. La Serna's 9,000 Royalists swept down the hill, but the Royalist attack was poorly coordinated. Through precise counterattacks, Sucre defeated the Royalists in detail. La Serna, along with most of the Royalist army, surrendered. The battle of Ayacucho sealed Patriot victory in Peru and in the Americas.

William Miller

William Miller was a British officer who entered the service of Río de la Plata. He arrived in Buenos Aires in 1817 with a captain's commission and departed in 1826 a general of Peru, having served under José San Martín, Thomas Cochrane, and Simón Bolívar. During his service Miller commanded artillery, marines, guerrillas, and cavalry. He fought in pitched battles, raids, and in command of his own independent campaigns. Upon his return to England in 1826 he collaborated with his brother, John, to write his memoirs.

Miller was born in Wingham, Kent on December 2, 1795. "Very tall and handsome, of winning address" (Lee 1894: 427), Miller joined the Royal Artillery on January 1, 1811. He was assigned to the field train in Wellington's army and saw action at Ciudad Rodrigo, Badajoz, San Sebastián, Vitoria, and Bayonne. With the conclusion of fighting in Europe, Miller joined the British forces in North America commanding a company of Royal Engineers. He was at the battle of Bladensburg and was "within a few yards" of Major-General Robert Ross when the latter was killed at the battle of North Point on September 12, 1814 (Markham 1862: 521). He sailed on to New Orleans, but it is not clear whether he saw action in that campaign.

Like many other British veterans, the end of the Napoleonic Wars found Miller drifting on half-pay with no plan for the future. Turning down an opportunity to become a partner in a French mercantile house, he decided to join the Patriot cause in South America. He sailed to Buenos Aires in August 1817 and fell in with well-connected British merchants. Miller was briefly tempted to join them until the wife of one told him "were I a young man, I would never abandon the career of glory for the sak of gain" (Miller 1829: I.139).

During this time Miller took a riding tour of the region around Buenos Aires. He stumbled across a maltreated group of 38 Spanish officers, taken prisoner in 1814 and held in a small ghost town. An unnamed major made an especially strong impression. "His ghastly countenance, long beard, and squalid figure, rendered him the picture of wretchedness ... His eyes had become diseased; and an old sack was hung

General William Miller, 1829, artist unknown. Miller was both a handsome man and fearless leader. Here he is dressed as a Peruvian general, but with a poncho covering his uniform and the stitched leather trousers characteristic of "Montoneros," as Peruvian guerrillas were called. Both were symbols of his preference for the common soldiers over their Creole officers. (From *Memoirs of General Miller*)

up as a curtain to shield them from the glare of the day." Miller gave the major some tea and spent the night with the group. They discovered they shared common acquaintances from the Peninsula. Miller took comfort in knowing he had made the "inmates forgetful, for a few hours, of their situation" (Miller 1829: I.146).

During his service, Miller repeatedly encountered Royalist officers he knew from the Peninsula. In 1818 he was saved from execution by the intercession of two Spanish officers with whom he shared mutual friends, and he traded letters with Jerónimo Valdés, one of the leading Spanish generals in Peru. During the 1824 campaign Valdés, upon learning Miller was so poor he was forced to chew coca leaves like a common soldier, sent him a box of Cuban cigars. Such Old World chivalry took the edge off a war whose brutality Miller freely acknowledged. In January 1818 Miller joined San Martín's army. His first impression was mixed:

The appearance of the troops …was not calculated to produce a favourable impression upon the mind of a superficial observer … Yet the composition of the army of the Andes was good, and although the dress of the soldiers was unsightly, they were well armed, tolerably well disciplined, and very enthusiastic. National airs and hymns to liberty were heard throughout the encampment every evening till a late hour. (Miller 1829: I.176)

Miller recorded many observations on the soldiers he commanded across his career. Most of them were black, Indian, or Mestizo. Miller's paternalistic descriptions of his men nevertheless challenged the racist stereotypes of the period:

The privates … were Creole negroes … by becoming soldiers, they obtained their freedom. They were distinguished throughout the war for their valor, constancy and patriotism. They were docile, easy to instruct, and devotedly attached to their officers. Many were remarkable for their intelligence, cleanliness, and good conduct. They went through their evolutions exceedingly well,

and it was generally allowed that they marched better than the corps formed of whites. (Miller 1829: I.271)

Miller was made captain and attached to the artillery, whose skill he quickly came to appreciate:

South American artillery can with ease perform a march of fifty or sixty miles a day for many days successively … If a horse knocks up on the march, one of the gunners rides up with a fresh one, and … takes the place of the jaded animal without the party slackening its march … Every gunner is competent to repair, or even make a harness … All were taught the horse-artillery, cavalry, and infantry exercises; and being all equally good horsemen, no difficulty or confusion arose out of this complexity of arms. (Miller 1829: I.173)

He thought even more highly of the cavalry:

To hear Creole officers speak of their cavalry as comparable with the finest in Europe was calculated to excite a smile in a newly arrived European, who, at first sight, would consider the comparison preposterous; but when his eye had become accustomed to the poncho and the slovenly appearance of the men, and he had seen them in action, he would then readily acknowledge that no European cavalry could cope with gaucho lancers, throughout a campaign, on South American ground. (Miller 1829: I.175)

Miller's first South American battle was at Cancha Rayada on March 19, 1818. His unit was in the thick of the action, but his account only mentions being "fortunate enough to save two guns" during the Patriot retreat (Miller 1829: I.182). He may have performed poorly, as after the battle San Martín transferred him to Valparaíso, where he was given command of a company of marines on board a newly purchased Chilean frigate:

She was officered principally by Englishmen. Her ship's company was composed of one

Revista de Rancagua, 1872, by Juan Manuel Blanes (1830–1901). In this depiction of San Martín reviewing the 8th Infantry Regiment, which Miller commanded in Peru, the unit is inaccurately shown in red coats – it wore blue. The red coats belonged to a second 8th Regiment serving in another division. (Museo Histórico Nacional, Argentina)

hundred foreign seamen, two hundred and fifty Chilenos, most of whom had never before been afloat … The Europeans had just before received bounty money, and, of all the ship's company, were, from inebriety, the least efficient, whilst hardly a naval officer could give an order in the Spanish language. (Miller 1829: I.188)

Despite the rocky beginning, the small Chilean navy soon proved to be a formidable force and, as he could speak Spanish, Miller became an important member of the squadron. He was promoted to major and given command of all the marines.

Miller led from the front and by example. His courage became legendary, but constant exposure to danger resulted in 26 wounds, many life-threatening. During a shore raid in November 1819 he was caught in a Royalist volley: "A musket-ball wounded him in the right arm; another permanently disabled his left hand; a third ball entered his chest, and, fracturing a rib, passed out the back. His recovery was despaired of" (Miller 1829: I.236). Still recovering 11 weeks later, he led shore parties in the assault on Valdivia harbor on February 3–4, 1820. He was so

weak he had to be carried, and afterwards was sent to Santiago, where he convalesced for another five months. He then joined the United Army and campaigned until the end of the war in Peru. His memoirs are filled with accounts of combats large and small, but his account of the battle of Ayacucho is so filled with insights to the period that it is worth quoting at length:

The gallant Cordova placed himself about 15 yards in front of his division, formed into four parallel columns with the cavalry in the intervals. Having dismounted, he plunged his sword into the heart of his charger, and turning to the troops, exclaimed, "There lies my last horse; I have now no means of escape, and we must fight it out together!" … These words were heard distinctly throughout the columns, which,

Guerrillero peruano de la campaña de la independencia, no date, anonymous. Between 1821 and 1824 Miller frequently organized and commanded groups of "Montoneros". Miller's empathy with the lower castes made him highly effective as a recruiter and beloved by his men. (Museo Histórico Militar Real Felipe, Peru)

inspired by the gallant bearing of their leader, moved to the attack in the finest possible order. The Spaniards stood firmly and full of apparent confidence … The hostile bayonets crossed, and for three or four minutes the two parties struggled together, so as to leave it doubtful which would give way. At this moment the Colombian cavalry, headed by Colonel Silva, charged. This brave officer fell covered with wounds, but the intrepidity of the onset was irresistible. The Royalists lost ground, and were driven back with great slaughter. The vice-king was wounded and taken prisoner. As the fugitives climbed the sides of Condorkanki, the Patriots, who had deployed, kept up a well-directed fire, and numbers of the enemy were seen to drop and roll down, till their progress was arrested by the brush-wood, or some jutting crag.

At the dawn of day, the Royalist division Valdez [sic] commenced a detour of nearly a league. Descending the sides of Condorkanki on the north, Valdez had placed himself on the left of the Patriots at musket-shot distance, separated by a ravine. At the important moment of the battle, just described, he opened a heavy fire from four field pieces and a battalion in extended files. By this, he obliged two battalions of the Peruvian division La Mar to fall back. The Colombian battalion [V]argas, sent to support the Peruvian division, also began to give way. Two Royalist battalions crossed the deep ravine … and advanced in double quick

time in pursuit of the retiring Patriots. At this critical juncture, Miller took upon himself to lead the hussars of Junin against the victorious Spaniards, and by a timely charge drove them back, and followed them across the ravine, by which time he was supported by the Granaderos a Caballo [horse grenadiers] and by the division La Mar, which had rallied. The brave Colonel Plaza crossed the ravine at the head of the legion on the left. Lieutenant-Colonel Moran, at the head of the battalion [V]argas, made a similar movement on the right of the cavalry. These two battalions and the cavalry, mutually supporting and rivaling each other in valour, repeated their charges with such resolution, that the division Valdez was broken; its artillery taken; its cavalry obliged to fly in disorder; and its infantry dispersed.
(Miller 1829: II.198)

When the war ended, Miller sailed for home. He returned to Peru in 1830, resuming his rank of general. Peru was in a period of civil war and Miller resigned his command twice, leaving Peru in 1836. He visited Hawaii on his way back to Britain, having met King Kamehameha III in 1831, and was appointed British Consul General in the Pacific in 1843. He returned to Peru as a private citizen in 1859 and died there in 1861. He is buried in the Pantheon of Heroes in Lima.

Anarchy and opportunity

Spain

Ferdinand VII was restored to the Spanish throne in early 1814, greeted by cheering mobs anticipating an era of peace and stability. Support for the 1812 Constitution faded, and Ferdinand dissolved the Cortes and rescinded the constitution. Conservatives were overjoyed by the return to absolute monarchy and reinstitution of the Inquisition. Despite the occasional harsh speech, Liberals reacted with almost uniform acquiescence despite being removed from office, imprisoned or otherwise marginalized.

Ferdinand and his new ministers saw crushing the rebellions in America as the keystone to reasserting Ferdinand's authority and rebuilding the economy. With the colonies firmly under control, the monopoly trade system would generate revenues for government and rejuvenate all sectors of the economy. The half measures of the Cortes were rejected in favor of full military reconquest, but the realities of outfitting the required expeditions forced the government to face the grim financial situation at home. British war subsidies ceased and there was no other base of revenue. In 1814 Spain ran a deficit of 60 million reales. In 1816 the deficit was 453,950,653 reales. Ferdinand's ministers eliminated all non-essential governmental

Triunfo de libertad Española, no date, anonymous. On July 7, 1822 the Royal Guard mutinied against Spain's Constitutional government, only to be defeated by units of the Madrid militia. The other European powers responded by authorizing a full-scale French intervention and Ferdinand VII's second restoration to absolute power. (Real Biblioteca del Palacio Real, Spain)

workers and slashed the bloated officer corps, in both cases without regard to the talent or service record of the individuals involved. They introduced a variety of taxes, donations and loans, many of them forced. Often these revenue-generating schemes overlapped. For example, shipyards were not only required to provide much-needed transports for the expeditions, but they were forced to pay for their docking and maintenance until needed. When the ships returned to private service, a 1 percent war levy was added to the standard cargo taxes. Similar taxes were spread throughout the system, affecting every corner of society.

Ferdinand's heavy-handed measures alienated many, and his moniker "The Desired One," uttered with rapturous anticipation in 1808, became a term of bitter irony. Liberal opposition reignited among the elite, while economic misery animated the masses. Tax evasion became a common pastime and political statement at all levels of society. Among the 20,000 soldiers gathered in squalid cantonments at Cádiz, the blatant corruption displayed by government officials and contractors provided the fuel of rebellion in 1820. Ferdinand was compelled to reinstitute both the 1812 Constitution and the Cortes.

To secure popular support for his insurrection, one of Colonel Rafael del Riego's first promises was to cut all taxes by 50 percent. This severely hampered the new Liberal government, as it meant it could afford even less than the restored monarchy. The second issue was that the 1812 Constitution gave Ferdinand considerable powers in appointing ministers and advisors – powers that Ferdinand used to delay, disrupt, and discredit Liberal government at every opportunity. Finally, the Liberals themselves fell into factions over how to best implement representative government. The result was three years of dithering that worsened the situation in the colonies and in the economy. In late 1822, Ferdinand seized a pan-European offer of restoration behind the force of a 100,000-man French army. When the French entered the country

Rafael del Riego, c. 1814–23, anonymous. Rafael del Riego was an undistinguished veteran of the Peninsular War, best known for being twice taken prisoner by the French, who was nevertheless retained by Ferdinand VII. Given command of the Asturias Regiment, he led the Cadiz uprising of 1820 that led to the restoration of the Cortes. (Museo Romántico, Spain)

in April 1823, they encountered only sporadic resistance. Spain was returned to monarchial rule.

Ferdinand's second restoration made his first seem mild by comparison. Hundreds of Liberals were executed – most notably Riego, who was hanged in a public square on November 7, 1823. Extreme measures were implemented across the social spectrum, including in the press and the arts, enforced by the Inquisition. In 1797 there were 2,705 Inquisitors in Spain; in 1826 there were 22,000 (Delmar 1875: 303). By this time Ferdinand's sole goal appears to have simply been to consolidate Bourbon rule and stamp out any trace of republican sentiment. Matters of economy, colonies, war or peace only mattered so much as they forwarded that goal.

International diplomacy

Both sides sought British support during the war. The government of Prime Minister William Pitt (the Younger) had provided some encouragement to Miranda's schemes in the early 1800s and the subsequent government under Lord Portland had been on the verge of launching an expedition to South America when the French invaded Spain. With Spain suddenly an ally, Britain adopted a policy of neutrality. Britain desired free trade with the Americas, and the ambiguity of supplying goods during a time of war allowed Britain to substantially increase direct trade with the colonies, despite the official continuation of the Spanish monopoly system.

As the wars progressed, so did pressures on British policy. The new Patriot governments sent representatives seeking official recognition, while Spain became more assertive as the Peninsular War ended. In 1815 Spain, knowing perfectly well what the British were after, offered exclusive trading rights if the British mediated the end of the rebellions. Britain demurred. The offer presented advantages if negotiations succeeded, but would irreparably harm Britain's position should they fail. As one minister put it, "We ought ... neither to encourage the immediate independence, nor to discourage the eventual independence, either of the whole, or of any part of Spanish America" (Bethel 1985: III.200).

Britain did, however, mediate between Portugal and Spain over the Banda Oriental. This had more to do with Continental politics than any colonial concern. The first mediation occurred in 1811, when Portuguese troops occupied the Banda Oriental at Spanish request. The Peninsular campaign was undecided and Britain could not afford a rupture between the ancient rivals. The Portuguese position was weak as Royalists still occupied Montevideo, and Portugal was reliant upon British arms at home. King John VI withdrew. The second mediation came in 1817. This time Portugal refused to withdraw on the grounds that

Spain had lost the territory and therefore had no claim against Portugal. The troops remained.

British neutrality was tested in 1817 and 1818 when Patriot agents began openly purchasing surplus military stores and recruiting British troops. The alliance with Spain specifically forbade such dealings, and Spanish complaints became impossible to ignore. When a wild public-house melee between two rival bands of mercenaries made it into the papers, the government was finally compelled to act. The Foreign Enlistment Act was passed in 1819, outlawing service in the Patriot armies. Goods, however, continued to flow unimpeded, often being channeled through neutral ports.

Like Britain, the United States was officially neutral. In reality the USA had long coveted Spain's North American territory, and the wars provided cover to act. In 1811 Bernardo Gutiérrez de Lara, a Patriot agent, traveled to Washington, DC. He sought American intervention in New Spain. He was warmly received by President James Madison, but ultimately left empty-handed. It was made clear to him, however, that the US would in no way impede his efforts. Accordingly, he went to the border town of Natchitoches and assembled a small army of American filibusters led by Augustus Magee, a US Army officer stationed in the area. This Anglo force campaigned alongside Tejano Patriots in 1812 and 1813, fighting several battles and briefly establishing an independent Texan republic before being defeated at the battle of Medina on August 18, 1813.

The Magee–Gutiérrez Expedition was not the only example where US citizens engaged in hostilities against Spain. In 1817 Gregor MacGregor, a Scottish adventurer who had served in the Venezuelan Patriot army, recruited a small expedition in the United States and seized Amelia Island, which was part of Spanish Florida. Exiled Spanish guerrilla hero Francisco Mina used Baltimore and New Orleans as staging grounds for an expedition against Mexico in 1817. A much

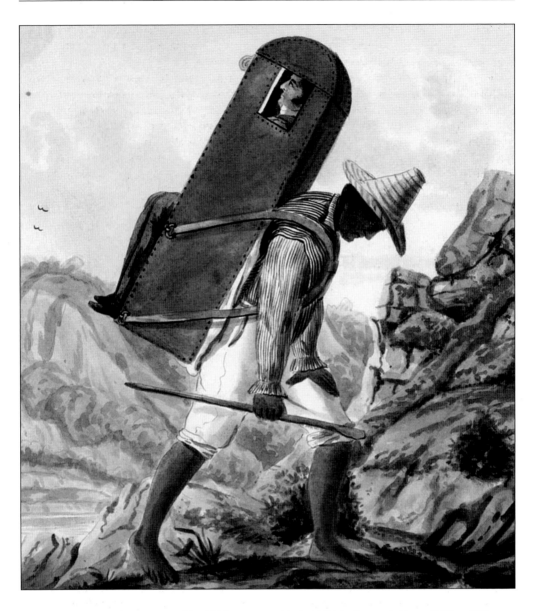

more serious incursion occurred in 1818 when US General Andrew Jackson entered Florida with 2,800 US troops and 1,400 Creek Indian allies as part of the First Seminole War (1814–19). Jackson went so far as to attack the small Spanish garrison at Pensacola, forcing its surrender. Spain was so weak that after a brief diplomatic row the government negotiated the sale of Florida to the United States in 1819. The resulting treaty also clarified the boundaries of the Louisiana Purchase, which soon demarcated the border between the USA and Mexico.

Untitled, 1828, by Auguste le Moyne (1800–c. 1880). Auguste le Moyne was a French diplomat who served in Colombia from 1828 until 1839. He painted many scenes of everyday Colombian life. Here, an unfortunate Indian or Mestizo toils as a human porter. Both Patriots and Royalists attempted to channel resentment of white oppression in their recruiting efforts. (Museo Nacional de Colombia)

Once Mexico declared independence, neutrality fell by the wayside. The United States recognized Gran Colombia on June 19, 1822, Mexico on December 12, 1822 and Chile and Río de la Plata on January 27, 1823.

In response to fears that the French restoration of Ferdinand VII signaled an impending French intervention in the Americas, the United States announced the Monroe Doctrine on December 2, 1823. The document reasserted Patriot independence and announced that "any interposition for the purpose of oppressing them, or controlling in any other manner their destiny" would be considered an "unfriendly" action against the United States. While hardly the "America's Backyard" announcement it later came to represent, it was the strongest statement on behalf of the Patriot cause by an outside power during the wars.

Britain and the United States were not the only countries that took interest in Spain's colonial difficulties. All of the European powers involved themselves in the issue, for varying reasons. Russia proved to be Spain's most stalwart ally, going so far as to sell her eight warships in 1817. All of the powers, however, felt Spain's position was increasingly weak, and urged concessions in matters of trade and colonial equality. As de facto independence emerged in the new countries, the European interests shifted into achieving a peaceful transition that preserved the old order at home. As part of this, France received the blessings of the other powers to invade Spain in 1823 with the object of restoring Ferdinand to absolute monarchy. By returning Ferdinand to power, France not only wished to reaffirm Bourbon rule, but intended to force Ferdinand to convene a full European Congress on the issue of South America, where he would be forced to give up his claims.

The colonies

People living in the colonies suffered all the calamities of war: food, horses, and supplies requisitioned by passing armies, banditry by deserters and outlaws, high taxes, and repressive military government in the zone of conflict. There were two areas, however, where the experiences of the wars of independence were exceptional: the "War to the Death" and the role of the war in emancipating slaves.

When Bolívar issued his infamous "War to the Death" decree in 1813, he deliberately isolated the Peninsulare population through a policy of institutionalized terrorism. While historians have debated whether the policy was rooted in Spanish tradition or was Bolívar's unique invention, the effect was to codify, even reward, barbarism on a mass scale. The subsequent cruelties unleashed on both sides horrified contemporary observers. George Chesterton, a veteran of both the Peninsular War and War of 1812, witnessed one "War to the Death" sacrifice while serving the Patriot cause:

In the dead of night they were conducted to a contiguous spot, and were there pierced by the rude spears of the natives, until they died covered by countless wounds. I subsequently went to the fatal spot ... and looked with horror upon the mangled corpse of that young Spanish captain, whom I had seen so recently smiling at our passing jokes. That scene was a death-blow to all my past enthusiasm ... and several officers ... participating with me in the detestation for cold-blooded butchery, conspired from that moment to elude this detested service. (Chesterton 1853: II.88)

At times the tales undoubtedly drift into lurid propaganda, either through embellishment or deliberate falsification, but there is no doubt that extreme acts of depravity were regular occurrences. One tale of many serves to illustrate the point. José Tomás Boves, a man who gained a truly terrible reputation, had been fought to a standstill in front of Valencia. He offered terms to the garrison, swearing upon the Holy Eucharist to spare their lives and property. The garrison accepted. The men and women of the town were separated, with the men placed under guard. "The following day he invited the prominent citizens and the officers of the garrison to eat with him, and that same night he invited their wives to a ball," wrote Daniel O'Leary, one of Bolívar's aides:

Batalla de Chacabuco, 1909, by Pedro Subercaseaux (1880–1956). For the most part armies in Spanish America were quite small by European standards. Their size, along with the vast geographical distances over which they operated, made the skills of the individual commander paramount. (Museo de Armas de la Nación, Argentina; photograph by René Chartrand)

When the ladies arrived, he gave secret orders to his executioners for the death of their victims. An hour later all of them had been murdered. Meanwhile, the ladies continued dancing until midnight, and Boves joked with them about the absence of their loved ones. They came face to face with the stark reality of their misfortune when they returned to their homes. (O'Leary 1970: 69)

The story was corroborated by Juan Manuel Cajigal, Captain General of Venezuela, who lamented in 1819 that Boves used "robbery ... assassination, rape and all manner of depravations" as an inducement to enlistment (Cajigal 1960: 133).

"War to the Death" primarily affected whites. Bolívar's decree specifically exempted Americans of any race, while Boves' rage was focused against Creoles. One of Bolívar's officers, seeking to terrorize a village, was disappointed to find the only Spaniards were two elderly men in their seventies. He killed them both with his own sword. While a horrific deed in its own right, the commander could have just as easily committed atrocities against the entire town on grounds of being Royalist. This limitation reflects another reality of the war: the necessity of support from the lower castes

to supply the manpower for each army. Venezuela alone lost an estimated 262,000 inhabitants during the wars, out of a total population of about 1 million. In 1810 Caracas had a population of 50,000; in 1816 it was 21,000. In Cumaná the population declined from 16,000 to 5,236 during the same period. Attrition rates in the armies were equally dramatic. Desertion was endemic on both sides, and climate and disease decimated armies before they could even be brought to action. Non-white prisoners were often given the choice of joining their captor's army or being sent to a prison fortress, and both sides aggressively expanded their recruitment efforts among Indian and slave populations.

Slavery had a different character within the Spanish caste system compared to the French, British, or American versions. While every bit as violent and cruel as those other examples, in the Spanish system slaves could engage in outside economic activity, accumulate money, and buy their freedom. Free blacks and Pardos had long been accepted in the colonial militias. This theoretical fluidity between free and slave status, and the general acceptance of slavery as a legal concept rather than some kind of natural order, made the recruitment of slave soldiers less controversial than it would have been in other areas. The main objections to using slave soldiers were fear of race war and compensation for the slave owners. The realities of war soon pushed such concerns into the background, and ex-slaves became a vital component to the armies on both sides. In just one example, at the battle of Chacabuco in 1817, two-thirds of the Patriot infantry were ex-slaves.

Hidalgo abolished slavery in 1810, but his subsequent defeat meant that his decree carried no weight. As a condition of sanctuary during his exiles in Haiti, Bolívar declared "there will be no more slaves in Venezuela, except those who wish to be slaves" (quoted in Blanchard 2008: 66). He subsequently made great use of ex-slaves in his army. Among the new Patriot countries

Mexico abolished slavery in 1820, although enforcement was problematic, and Chile followed in 1823. In the other countries, emancipation was limited to either personal freedom for those who served or to "free womb" laws, first introduced in Río de la Plata in 1813, that decreed all children, regardless of their parent's status, were either born free or would be automatically freed at a certain age. These half-measures led to heartbreaking scenes after the wars, as many people were returned to bondage. Some were able to petition the government or even challenge their owner's claims in court, but most were powerless. As Maria Josefa Ramirez, a camp follower whose husband, also a slave, had served in both the Royalist and Patriot armies, remarked at her trial: "the poor and unfortunate are regularly the plaything of the powerful, because the former can only with difficulty demonstrate to those who govern the latter's … insults" (quoted in Blanchard 2008: 158). Nevertheless, the gains made during Independence were permanent – by 1853 every ex-Spanish colony had eliminated the institution entirely.

Francisco José de Caldas

In 1810 Francisco José de Caldas was one of the leading scientists in New Granada. Like most people, Caldas was more interested in his career and family than politics. In a few short years, however, politics, and the conflicts that arose from them, would destroy everything he had ever done.

Caldas was born in Popayán, New Granada on October 4, 1768 to a modestly successful Creole family. As a child he attended the Seminario Mayor de Popayán, where he became enchanted by mathematics. Outside of Bogotá, the seminary was the only school in the viceroyalty that taught mathematics. Caldas gave a hint of the tensions between the Church and the Enlightenment when he wrote of how his teacher, José Félix de Restrepo, exposed him to the topic: "Under his guidance I applied myself to the study of arithmetic, geometry, trigonometry, algebra and experimental physics, because our philosophy class was really a course in physics and mathematics" (quoted in Appel 1994: 3). Like many other young men, Caldas' father insisted his son drop such frivolous subjects and study law. Caldas was sent to school in Bogotá. He graduated in 1793 and returned to Popayán, where he taught law and looked after the legal aspects of the family's landholdings.

At some point in the next couple of years, Caldas fell ill. As part of his treatment, his doctors ordered him to give up all mental exertions. Caldas quit his practice and became a traveling merchant. It only took Caldas a couple of months before he realized his real calling was science. In 1796 he went to Bogotá, bought whatever scientific instruments he could find, and immersed himself in the fields of botany, astronomy, and geography. Over the next 14 years he rose from being an untrained, unknown amateur to one of the colony's foremost intellectuals. His greatest contribution was independently discovering the Hypersometric Principle – the relationship between altitude and the temperature at which water boils – but he also made important strides in understanding the cinchona plant, used in making quinine, and cartography. By 1810 he was director of the Astronomical Observatory in Bogotá and a senior member of the Botanical Expedition, one of the leading lights of the Enlightenment in New Granada. He had wealthy patrons who covered his financial needs and was in the process of arranging a marriage with Manuela Barahona, niece of an old friend from Popayán.

Francisco José de Caldas, c. 1881–87, by Rodriguez. Caldas rose from an undistinguished background to become one of the leading South American scientists of his day. He dreamed of being included in the company of the German explorer Alexander von Humboldt and establishing Bogotá as a center of knowledge. (Banco de la República de Colombia)

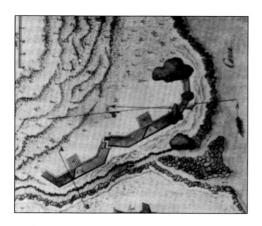

Fuerte de Arquia, 1813, by Francisco José de Caldas.
A plan, drawn in his own hand, of one of the forts
Caldas designed for Antioquia. (Casa museo
Francisco José de Caldas, Colombia)

Due to his relationships with many
key revolutionaries, historians have
debated what role, if any, Caldas played
in establishing the July 1810 junta. Caldas
maintained a friendly relationship with
Viceroy Amar, and just four months before
the junta took power had sent copies of his
scientific journal, *El Seminario del Nuevo Reino
de Granada*, to Spain, seeking government
recognition and financial support for the
Observatory. Most likely any involvement
was simple guilt by association. For example,
Caldas' late mentor, José Celestino Mutis,
had been imprisoned in the 1790s for
disseminating copies of *The Rights of Man*.
Nevertheless, once the junta was installed,
Caldas adapted to the situation. Since he
already published a scientific journal, he
volunteered to publish a political paper
called the *Diário Político*. It was a short-lived
paper that operated for less than half a year.

During this period, Caldas struggled to
keep both the Observatory and the Botanical
Expedition functioning. He wrote a bitter
letter to the first president of Cundinamarca,
accusing him of having "nearly ruined"
both, presumably through lack of funding.
In addition to the *Semanario*, he produced
scientific almanacs for 1811 and 1812. In
the 1812 almanac he advocated extending
independence into the realm of Inquisitional

censorship. "If we have shaken off the
political yoke of Europe," he wrote, "let
us also shake off that scientific dependence
that degrades us and that maintains us in
a literary infancy more ignominious than
slavery" (quoted in Appel 1994: 109).

The year 1812 was a pivotal one for
Caldas. In March President Nariño, whom
Caldas once characterized as "crazy," sent
an expedition against the Congress of the
United Provinces. Caldas was commissioned
a captain and put in charge of a detachment
of engineers. It is not certain if Caldas
volunteered for service or was pressured
into it. He and Manuela had just had their
first child, a son named Liborio, in July
1811, and Caldas had never shown any
interest in military matters. He proved to be
a half-hearted soldier at best. On the march
to Tunja he wrote "in the midst of the crisis
I observe, calculate and draw, and only the
current of politics makes me comment
on things other than geography and
astronomy" (quoted in Appel 1994: 110).
When the commander of the expedition,
Colonel Antonio Baraya, defected to the
Federalist Congress, Caldas joined him,
decrying Nariño as "a tyrant in disguise ...
who called himself free and humane, and in
1794 published the Rights of Man, only to
scandalously violate them in 1812" (quoted
in Appel 1994: 111). It is difficult to know
how deeply Caldas' sentiments ran. His
correspondence was prone to hyperbole,
usually to obtain funding for his scientific
efforts. He may have simply concluded that
with Baraya's defection his new patrons would
be the Congress in Tunja. Calculated or sincere,
he understood the risks, writing Manuela to
"hide yourself along with my papers and
books" (quoted in Appel 1994: 111).

At the end of the year, Bayara laid siege to
Bogotá. Caldas had been given to understand
that Manuela and Liborio had been
imprisoned by Nariño. He wrote an angry
letter to Nariño stating "You may torture,
threaten and decapitate this innocent,
virtuous woman and do the same to my little
son ... If they die ... they will die with honor
and virtue ... This innocent blood you are

about to shed will call down the awful vengeance of Heaven upon you" (quoted in Blossom 1967: 96). Nariño replied: "your wife came to my house along with the other ladies," reportedly under arrest:

They deplored the misfortunes about to be visited upon us and how they were the first victims whom inhuman husbands, fathers, and sons were about to immolate ... You are now avenging yourselves for hurts which exist solely in your imagination ... if you wish to end this civil war ... you can do so by adding your influence to the calming of base passions ... that we should embrace again as brothers, spouses, fathers, sons. (Quoted in Blossom 1967: 97)

Nariño's letter must have affected Caldas – he voted against attacking Bogotá. The vote went against him. Baraya attacked and was routed.

The defeat at Bogotá devastated Caldas. He was disgusted by the civil war and resigned his commission. "Now I am not an engineer, now I am not an official of the Union, I am simply F. J. de Caldas and nothing more; with this mail I have sent my resignation and with four lines acquired my true necessities – my peace, my liberty, my mathematics and my tranquility" (quoted in Appel 1994: 113). He also resigned his positions in Bogotá, stating "the Observatory has come to an end for me" (quoted in Appel 1994: 113). He decided to leave the country entirely, writing to Manuela "It is necessary, my child, to abandon this nation ... and to seek asylum far from here where one neither sees crowns, nor hears the name of kings" (quoted in Appel 1994: 113). Caldas spent the first half of 1813 in Cartago, a town in Antioquia province, just west of Cundinamaraca, which had stayed neutral in the civil war. He was waiting for Manuela, who at this time must have told him of giving birth to his daughter, probably conceived when he left in early 1812.

El "quintamiento" de Popayán, 1816, by José María Espinosa (1796–1883). Espinosa drew this eyewitness sketch of a Royalist firing squad executing Patriot prisoners at the same prison where Caldas was detained. Caldas may have even heard these shots as he awaited his own fate. (Casa Museo del 20 de Julio, 1810, Colombia)

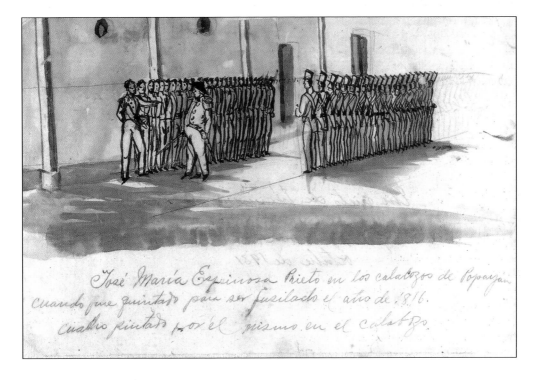

She had died during the siege, less than one month old.

Given his reference to a land without crowns, it seems Caldas meant to flee to the United States. He ended up staying in Antioquia. Antioquia had avoided the civil war, but was threatened by Royalist forces in Pasto and Popayán. The government offered Caldas a commission as a colonel in charge of engineering which, having no other options, he accepted. After a few months building a series of fortifications, he was sent to establish a school for engineering cadets. It was hardly the Botanical Expedition or Observatory, but at least it was science. As Caldas wrote: "I have had to dedicate myself to the study of fortifications and artillery. It is true that these horrible sciences have their charms, but nothing of the majesty and grandeur of the skies. Fortunately, they are well-defined sciences so that two or three months of methodic study are enough to master them" (quoted in Appel 1994: 115). The school's curriculum reflected Caldas' strengths: mathematics, geography, and cartography. Caldas spent two years in Antioquia. Besides his school, he put his scientific skills to use establishing a nitrate mill for the making of gunpowder as well as foundries for both cannon and muskets. He also set up a mint for the pressing of coins. While he and Manuela suffered the loss of Liborio, they had another daughter, Juliana. Another was on the way when the Spanish arrived.

Caldas returned to Bogotá with his family in November 1815. His cousin had been named president of the United Provinces, and Caldas may have imagined an opening to reclaim his beloved Observatory. Whatever the reason, it was a short-lived dream, as Cartagena fell to the Spanish in December. In March his cousin, with Royalist troops fast approaching, decided to flee to Popayán. Caldas, leaving Manuela and Juliana, went with him. During the journey south he appears to have realized his end was at hand. "Take care my dear child," he wrote her, "care for the education of Julianita and the child in your womb; teach them to fear God, and to be virtuous even though orphaned and poor" (quoted in Appel 1994: 119). With nowhere else to go, Caldas returned to his family home, where he was arrested in July 1816. Caldas' mother died in his arms when she visited him in prison on July 21. The local Royalist commander was moved by pity for Caldas and agreed to send him to live with a brother in Quito. Before the order could be executed, however, word arrived from Pablo Morillo that all prisoners were to be sent to Bogotá. Caldas sent a plea for clemency to Morillo's chief of staff. He noted that he had never actually fought Spain, listed his accomplishments for the Botanical Expedition and all the work yet to be done and closed with the plea: "… may your Excellency take pity on me, on my unfortunate family and save me for the King" (quoted in Appel 1994: 121). When Morillo was told of his plea, he is said to have responded "Spain does not need wise people." Caldas was shot in the back on October 29, 1816. Manuela and their children faded into historical obscurity with no one to chronicle their fate.

"The peoples are tired and want nothing but peace and order"

New Spain

New Spain was the first viceroyalty to achieve independence. It was also the last to fire shots against Spanish troops. In 1821 Agustín de Iturbide, a staunch Creole Royalist, was ordered to stamp out a recently resurgent guerrilla group led by Vicente Guerrero. Guerrero was an old officer of Morelos' – a simple man but a fearsome fighter and leader. After Morelos' death, he had continued fighting with a band of about 1,000 men. Iturbide was a good choice for eliminating him. He had led the cavalry charge that broke Morelos' army at Valladolid and had a reputation for mercilessly stamping out insurgency. However, instead of attacking Guerrero he opened negotiations.

Iturbide, along with many others, was profoundly distraught by the 1820 reinstitution of the Cortes in Spain. Both Absolutists and Constitutionalists in New Spain felt betrayed – Absolutists by the return of the Cortes, Constitutionalists by the insincerity of the Cortes toward their demands. Creoles in both camps sensed their interests now lay in independence. Iturbide offered Guerrero a deal of three guarantees in exchange for Guerrero's support: independence, loyalty to the Catholic Church and legal equality for all citizens. On the surface it looked similar to Morelos' agenda, and Guerrero accepted. Their newly combined army marched on

Entrada del Generalísimo Dn. Augustine de Yturbide à Megico el dia 27. Septiembre de 1821, no date, anonymous. Focusing on the frenzied joy that greeted Iturbide's theatrical ending of the war, this patriotic painting gives only hints of the dilapidated state of the city and the misery of its inhabitants. (Instituto Nacional de Estudios Históricos de las Revoluciones de México)

Agustín de Iturbide, 1865, by Primitivo Mirando. Usually portrayed as a great patriot who secured Mexican independence, Iturbide was a staunch monarchist committed to retaining all the privileged status of the Creole elite. Siding with the cause of independence was a means to outwit and defeat the insurgents at home and the liberals in Spain. (Museo Nacional de Historia, Mexico)

Mexico City. The country, exhausted by a decade of war, enthusiastically supported this breakthrough. On September 27, 1821 the army entered the capital unopposed. The new viceroy, Juan O'Donojú, offered Iturbide the keys to the city.

To the discomfort of many Patriots, Mexico was established as a constitutional monarchy. Ferdinand VII was given first right of refusal to the crown. After him, the crown was offered to a list of suitable European nobles. Ferdinand declined, objecting to the sole condition of the deal – he had to travel to Mexico to receive the crown. The Cortes flatly refused to allow any other royal to take the offer. A popular outburst in the city called in

favor of Iturbide. On July 21, 1822 he was crowned Augustine I, Emperor of Mexico.

Iturbide's reign was a chaotic mess. Seeking to win support and signal the end of the war, Iturbide dramatically lowered taxes. The masses approved, but government coffers, already depleted, were instantly drained. What money there was went to pay the grossly bloated officer corps, as Iturbide bought the army's support through copious commissions. Iturbide needed the army, as the national assembly agitated for republican rule. Events quickly spun out of control and a rebellion, led by Antonio López de Santa Anna (1794–1876), drove Iturbide into exile in 1823. The country became a republic. Subsequent governments, crippled by infighting, fared no better, and the depressed economy collapsed. In 1829 Guerrero became president in a wave of anti-Spanish riots, property seizures, and expulsions. Spain saw an opportunity to regain her lost colony under the guise of protecting Spanish lives and property, and 3,500 men were sent from Cuba to Tampico in July 1829. The Spanish barely advanced beyond their original landing zones. Within days a Mexican army of 3,750 men, led by the ever-opportunistic Santa Anna, arrived. They besieged the Spanish and stormed a key fort called La Barra on September 11, 1829. The Spanish commander sued for terms and returned to Cuba with 1,800 survivors.

New Granada

In February 1822 Bolívar put Páez in command of the Patriot forces in Venezuela, tasked with mopping up Royalist forces in the territory. With La Torre holed up in Puerto Cabello, the surrender of Cumaná, the last Royalist city in the east, in October 1821, and the declaration of independence of Panama that November, the quick end of hostilities appeared a foregone conclusion. However, Francisco Morales, Boves' old lieutenant, rallied support in Coro and by April 1822 raised a division of 2,500 men. Morales struck for Maracaibo, which he captured in early September. The Spanish navy achieved local dominance, allowing troops and supplies to move easily anywhere from Maracaibo to La Guaira, near Caracas. The Patriots decided the only way to defeat Morales was to cut his line of supply, which meant blockading Lake Maracaibo and defeating the Spanish navy should it appear.

On May 8, 1823 the Patriot fleet, commanded by José Prudencio Padilla, forced its way past Royalist forts that protected the entrance to Lake Maracaibo. Padilla defeated the Royalist flotilla defending the lake, but his fleet needed serious repairs. During this lull a Spanish fleet arrived from the Caribbean, docking in Maracaibo. Padilla was trapped. He refitted

Acción del castillo de Maracaibo, c. 1840, by José María Espinosa (1796–1883). This depiction of the battle of Maracaibo is a symbolic representation of monolithic Spanish power finally defeated by the Patriot navy. In reality Spanish ground forces peacefully surrendered both Maracaibo and Fort San Carlos on August 3, ten days after the crucial naval battle. (Museo Nacional de Colombia)

his ships as best he could and engaged the Spanish fleet on July 24. Eschewing traditional cannonades, Padilla sailed in close, ramming and boarding the Spanish vessels. It was a complete victory. Morales, holed up in one of the forts at the lake entrance, surrendered on August 3. In Puerto Cabello, Páez stormed the outlying fortifications on November 8. Holding only the inner fortress and with no hope of relief, the remaining Royalist garrison surrendered on November 23, ending the war in Venezuela.

Río de la Plata

When Montevideo fell to the Patriots on June 23, 1814, Portugal reasserted her old territorial claims. In August 1816 a 10,000-man army that included over 4,000 Peninsular veterans entered the country. Repeatedly defeating Artigas' outclassed Patriots, they quickly occupied Montevideo

New American nations

and, by 1820, controlled the entire territory. On July 18, 1821 the Banda Oriental was annexed by Portugal, becoming the province of Cisplatina. Artigas went into exile in Paraguay. In 1825 the United Provinces of Río de la Plata went to war with Imperial Brazil, which had achieved independence from Portugal in 1822, over Cisplatina. The United Provinces emerged victorious: in the peace that was negotiated under British mediation, Cisplatina achieved independence with the name of Uruguay.

Across the Río de la Plata the tensions between Centralists, known regionally as Unitarians, and Federalists burst into open conflict in 1818 when the Federalist League provinces of Santa Fe and Entre Ríos joined forces against the United Provinces. After a brief campaign the two sides declared a truce. Fighting broke out again in 1819 after the United Provinces passed a new constitution that reiterated Unitarian rule. Rondeau was named Supreme Director and ordered San

Batalla de Maipú, 1918, by Pedro Subercaseaux (1880–1956). Subercaseaux painted numerous versions of this battle. Here is a scene depicting the heroic stand the Spanish Burgos Regiment (in white) against the full weight of the Patriot attack. (Museo Histórico Nacional, Chile)

Martín's Army of the Andes and the Army of the North, again under Belgrano, to return and defend Buenos Aires. San Martín ignored him while the Army of the North mutinied. Rondeau was completely routed by the Federalist forces at the battle of Cepeda on February 1, 1820. The national government all but collapsed as each province followed its own leaders. However, the Royalists were preoccupied with the campaign in Peru, and did not attempt to exploit the situation beyond regional raids in Jujuy and Salta in 1821. The United Provinces and Federal League descended into a confusing swirl of civil wars until 1862, when the modern state of Argentina, under its first elected president, Bartolomé Mitre (1821–1906), finally emerged.

Peru

After the battle of Ayacucho, the Patriot army quickly occupied the rest of Royalist Peru. In January 1825 Sucre began a campaign against Olañeta, still holding out in Upper Peru. It was a quick campaign, as Olañeta's forces deserted or defected. Olañeta was killed trying to put down one of these rebellions at the battle of Tumulsa on April 1. Some accounts maintain the only shot fired in this battle was the one that felled Olañeta. Small bands of Royalists continued fighting as guerrillas, the last being defeated in 1829, but for all intents the campaign was over. The Republic of Bolivia was declared on August 6, 1825 with Sucre as the first president.

In Peru, the last Royalist outpost was the port fortress at Callao. After the Patriot garrison mutinied in 1824, it was replaced by a 2,280-man Royalist division commanded by José Ramón Rodil. Bolívar assigned a division to besiege the fort and an eight-ship squadron to blockade the harbor. Rodil, certain that Spanish reinforcements would inevitably arrive, grimly held out against all odds. Supplies ran out in the middle of 1825, but Rodil still refused to surrender. On January 3, 1826 the Patriots took a key outlying fort and, reluctantly, Rodil acknowledged defeat. Negotiations opened on January 11, and on

January 23 the garrison, reduced to only 400 men, formally capitulated. The 91 Spaniards in the garrison, including Rodil, were allowed to sail home, where they were received with honors and accolades.

San Martín's first report on the battle of Maipú read simply "The country is free." Perhaps, but it was far from secured. The Royalists had over 2,000 regulars in southern Chile, while an ill-fated expedition from Spain managed to land an additional 600 in October 1818. The Royalists launched a campaign mixing conventional and guerrilla warfare, joined in temporary alliance by the Arauca Indians, eternally hostile to European encroachment. For the next six years, a new era of "War to the Death" raged from Chillán to Chiloé. The Patriot advance was slow but inexorable and by 1826 all that remained was Chiloé Island. The Royalist garrison was led by Colonel Antonio Quintanilla, a talented veteran who had fought tirelessly for the Royalist cause since 1813. The garrison repelled a raid by Thomas Cochrane in 1820 and an invasion attempt led by General Ramón Freire in 1824. Freire invaded again on January 11, 1826. With 2,600 men, he defeated the 1,500 defenders on January 14. The island capitulated the next day. Although scattered bands of Royalist guerrillas held out into the 1840s, the war of independence had finally ended.

Conclusion and consequences

No great conference or treaty ended
the wars of independence. The defeat of
the individual viceregal armies and the
inability of Spain to project power caused a
gradual cessation of hostilities. The de facto
peace slowly formalized in the years after
Ferdinand VII's death in 1833 – Spain
recognized Mexico in 1836, Chile in 1844,
and Paraguay in 1880. At the end of the war,
both Spain and the new American countries
were devastated. Their political systems
were all on the verge of collapse and their
economies in shambles. Almost every nation

*Parte de Caracas destruida por el terremoto, c. 1842–45,
by Ferdinand Bellermann (1814–89). This painting
unintentionally reveals the extent of economic and
social devastation inflicted by the war of independence:
30 years after the great 1812 earthquake, portions of
Caracas had not yet been rebuilt. (Museos Estatales
Collection, Germany)*

was involved in civil war within ten years
of the end of the conflict, and many of the
nations fell upon each other over unresolved
territorial issues.

The new nations

The most promising immediate change
brought by independence was social
equality. The need for manpower had
quickly expanded the ranks of both
Royalists and Patriots beyond the Creole
and Peninsulares castes. Fueled in equal parts
by Enlightenment sentiment and military
desperation, Indians saw the end of forced
tribute and coerced-labor laws while slaves
enjoyed varying degrees of emancipation.
In the new countries, all citizens were legally
recognized as equal. Legal equality, however,

did not amount to practical equality. One of the initial Creole complaints was that they had been kept out of viceregal administrations. With independence, government posts were almost uniformly taken by Creoles. In Gran Colombia José Padilla, the Mulatto admiral and hero of Lake Maracaibo in 1823, agitated for greater inclusion of non-whites in both the economic and political spheres. Bolívar had him executed. It was a strong signal that Enlightenment ideals went only so far.

Even without violating the law, however, exploitation of non-whites continued. For example, after independence many Indian workers were not paid by wages but in individual land grants. These destroyed the communal bonds on which Indians traditionally depended and placed each individual landowner at the mercy of the holders of giant estates. The estate holders

Batalla de Sarandí, no date, by Esteban Garino (1911–). Wars continued to rage unabated across the former colonies for decades. The battle of Sarandí, fought on October 12, 1825, was a key Uruguayan victory over the forces of Brazil during the Cisplatine War (1825–28). (Museo Histórico Nacional, Uruguay)

became so powerful that they often replaced government in the daily lives of those in their region, and this power was a key element in the rise of the Caudillo. Caudillos had shown their influence during the wars, whether it be Güemes' Gauchos or Páez's Llaneros, and they played a central role in the post-independence civil wars.

One of the key goals for independence was trade liberalization. Creoles understood that the old Spanish monopoly was weighed heavily against them. They believed free, direct trade would increase the nation's wealth and their own profit. Unfortunately, they were wrong. Britain was by far the leading trade partner for the new nations, followed by the United States, France, and Spain. The advanced industrial development of Britain allowed it to unload surplus production through massive dumping in South American markets – that is, selling products at a loss. This increased South American trade deficits, undercut other trading nations, and led to the collapse of local industries that could not compete with the price or quality of British staples. On the export side, prices for South American goods, almost all raw materials, either went through

boom-and-bust cycles or experienced a long-term decline. However, there were regional successes. In the immediate post-war era, Venezuelan coffee and Mexican textile exports provided bright spots in otherwise bleak economic pictures. Peru secured a British monopoly on guano exports, control of which became a vital issue later in the century. The industry that benefitted most from liberalized trade was ranching. South America produced vast herds of cattle and the European market eagerly bought the surplus. Unfortunately, this was a rare exception to an overall cycle that led to bankrupting levels of debt and limited local economies.

Mining, arguably the key industry for most of the region, suffered dramatically in the postwar era. Although wartime damage to the mines themselves was limited, mine owners simply did not have the money for operations and maintenance. The case of Mexico illustrates the cycle that occurred across the region. Silver mining fell 75 percent between 1810 and 1818, and by the end of the war many mines were flooded or otherwise inoperable. A large number were sold to British companies; in 1826 a full one-third of Mexican mines had Cornish directors, in the hopes that they could be revived by British expertise. It took until the 1870s for the industry to recover, but this simply replaced silver revenues going to Spain with silver revenues going to Britain and, by then, the United States. In both the prewar and postwar economies Mexico's wealth ended up in foreign coffers. The echoes of these economic outcomes are still felt in the region's history of nationalizing key resources like oil, or the attempts to forge third-way economies and regional trading blocs as a counter to the various free-trade agreements demanded by economically dominant countries.

Politically, independence brought to the fore the conflict between Federalists and Centralists, now often referred to as Liberals and Conservatives, respectively. With the common Spanish enemy gone, the two sides immediately fell upon each other.

Governmental anarchy at best, and full civil war at worst, was the result. These civil wars continued into the 20th century, and the accompanying instability greatly hindered the development of almost every nation. When they weren't experiencing violent internal power struggles, the new nations were fighting each other. A depressing series of wars, especially between the nations in the southern half of South America, raged almost non-stop until the 1870s and 1880s.

Mexico

After Iturbide's overthrow, the Mexican government entered a decade of confusion as various factions — Federalists and Centralists, Creoles and Mestizos – attempted to mold the new republic to their interests. The fragility of the new government was a reflection of the anarchy across the land. A half-million people had died during the wars, and Mexico City experienced multiple outbreaks of yellow fever. Bandits roamed the roads, and the war severely affected economic production in every corner of the country. This chaos was exploited by newly arriving American settlers in Texas. To make up for the loss of the Peninsulare population, many of whom fled to Cuba or Spain, the Mexican government tried to attract new immigrants. Texas had proven particularly difficult to settle and Mexico was open to American migrants as long as they swore loyalty to their new home. The settlers injected new life into the region, but were quickly disgusted by the inefficient, at times barely functioning, government. The Americans thought, not without reason, that they could do a better job of it than the Mexicans, while Mexicans complained of the Americans taking over. The issue erupted in the Texas Revolution of 1835–36. Although Santa Anna signed a treaty granting Texan independence, the government in Mexico City refused to recognize it and continued to view Texas as a rebellious province. Tensions with the United States continued over the following decade. Things came to a head when the United States admitted Texas as a state on December 29, 1845. The Mexican government broke off diplomatic relations with the United States, and Mexico's humiliating defeat in the war that followed highlighted how weak post-independence Mexico had become.

Gran Colombia

The nation of Gran Colombia was entirely Bolívar's creation. Conceived in 1819, it may have been little more than an excuse for harnessing the resources of New Granada for the liberation of Venezuela. Regardless, by the end of the war Gran Colombia consisted of three confederated nations – Venezuela, Colombia, and Ecuador – and Bolívar's vision had grown to developing some kind of Pan-American nation, or at least a series of unified countries. This grandiose scheme quickly collapsed.

Bolívar had never been a good administrator. He was a charismatic

Simón Bolívar, 1830, by José María Espinosa (1796–1883). This sketch of Bolívar in the last days of his life shows the physical and emotional toll exacted by more than 15 years of military campaigns and political maneuvering. (Colección Sylvia Boulton)

leader, the prototypical Caudillo. Making himself the literal embodiment of the revolution, Bolívar quickly learned the Caudillo's core weakness: localized power. Bolívar had been able to bring all the Patriot generals to heel in 1817 because they were gathered in a limited geographic region. After this Bolívar had the loyalty of the army, which ensured him control of the government. Now that independence was achieved, the army began to fracture, and distance weakened the force of his commands. The Colombian troops in Bolivia and Peru ceased being viewed as liberators, while the troops in Gran Colombia reverted to the control of their respective leaders.

Daniel O'Leary, one of Bolívar's aides, wrote "in Colombia the individual was everything and the institutions meant nothing" (O'Leary 1970: 335). Bolívar discovered this as the rivalry between two of his old commanders, Santander and Páez, erupted into open conflict in late 1826. Bolívar was able to reassert control, but only by assuming dictatorial power that destroyed the government and left him with few allies; indeed, Santander was implicated in an attempt to assassinate Bolívar in 1828 and exiled. Isolated, ill, and almost universally despised as a tyrant whose time had come and gone, Bolívar accepted the inevitable and resigned from public office on January 20, 1830. His efforts to save Gran Colombia were in vain. Páez was declared president of an independent Venezuela on January 13, 1830. Ecuador followed by seceding in May. Bolívar died bitter and disillusioned in Santa Marta on December 17, 1830. Gran Colombia was formally abolished shortly thereafter.

After separation, Páez proved to be a capable leader. Although not always president, he maintained effective control of Venezuela until the late 1840s through alliance with the country's merchants. His personal popularity blunted complaints and Venezuela enjoyed an immediate post-war period of relative recovery, even growth. Conservatives also gained power in Colombia. Pasto rebelled in 1839, which spread into a Federalist movement across the south. This civil war lasted until 1842. Many more civil wars awaited Colombia in the second half of the century. Ecuador had its own problems, a weak economy, a lost war with Colombia in 1832, and a civil war in 1834 among them.

Peru, Bolivia, and Chile

Bolívar, despite his republican protestations, habitually proposed constitutions that amounted to little more than advisory legislators serving extremely powerful executives. He had many arguments for this form of government, some of which were widely held by contemporaries. His most powerful argument was that to move too quickly or too far towards a full democracy was simply to invite anarchy. In Bolívar's mind, a handful of wise men, freed from the pressures of public opinion, would guard the country's interest above all and steer the nation to prosperity. When he tried to implement this philosophy in Bolivia, he found that too many people had contributed too much to the cause simply to fall in line for what looked suspiciously like the old viceregal system in republican packaging. Bolívar's lieutenant Antonio José de Sucre had been made president of Bolivia. Sucre, an honest man who had no desire for power, was overwhelmed by local Caudillos. Unwilling to fight, he resigned the presidency in early 1828.

In Peru, the Bolívarian regime collapsed in 1827 with the election of Andres Santa Cruz. Within a matter of months he was replaced by José de la Mar, who commanded the Peruvian division at Ayacucho. De la Mar focused on reclaiming the traditionally Peruvian territories of Bolivia and southern Ecuador. All pretext of unity vanished as Sucre, along with the remaining Colombian troops, beat hasty retreats from Chuquisaca and Lima. De la Mar pressed his claims and war erupted between Peru and Gran Colombia in 1828. Sucre, commanding the Gran Colombian forces, defeated the larger

Retrato del Mariscal Antonio José de Sucre, 1895, by Arturo Michelena (1863–98). Sucre emerged as one of the war's most capable generals. Humble, humane, and endlessly loyal to Bolívar, he was assassinated by Bolívar's enemies on June 4, 1830 while riding to meet his wife in retirement. (Museo Gran Mariscal de Ayacucho, Venezuela)

Peruvian army at the battle of Tarqui on February 27, 1829. The defeat heralded the beginning of a long series of civil wars in Peru and Bolivia that culminated in the battle of Ingavi in 1841. For Sucre, Tarqui was his final act of public service. He was assassinated in 1830.

Chile was wracked by the familiar Liberal versus Conservative conflicts. O'Higgins, a Liberal, had been forced to step down in 1823. From 1823 until 1829 the country was ruled by several presidents, as the two sides struggled to adopt a lasting governmental framework. In 1829 Conservatives revolted over a disputed national election. The Conservatives won the battle of Lircay on April 17, 1830 and after exiling some Liberal leaders, most notably war hero Ramón Freire, both sides agreed to a settlement that provided a degree of stability unseen in the other countries. Peru emerged as Chile's primary rival. Chile fought a losing war against a Peru–Bolivia Confederation in 1836 over the regional balance of power and Peruvian support for a coup attempt by Freire.

United Provinces, Uruguay, and Paraguay

Nowhere were the immediate conflicts between Federalists and Centralists more pronounced than Río de la Plata. Embroiled in civil war years before Ayacucho, the various states of the Federal League and Río de la Plata continued to fight in a swirling series of shifting alliances until the battle of Pavón in 1861 brought about the emergence of modern Argentina. In the Banda Oriental a small group of Patriots instigated a revolution against Brazil, itself now independent of Portugal, in 1825. Río de la Plata joined the Patriots and defeated the Brazilians at the battle of Ituzaingó on February 20, 1827. British mediation ended the war in 1828 and the newly freed Banda Oriental became Uruguay, which

Asesinato del oficial Landáburu, no date, anonymous. On June 30, 1822 a group of the Royal Guard saluted Ferdinand VII by shouting "Long live the absolute King!" Mamerto Landáburu, a Constitutionalist officer, reprimanded them. The guards, allegedly encouraged by their officers, killed him on the steps of the royal palace. (Real Biblioteca del Palacio Real, Spain)

promptly fell into its own civil war. Only Paraguay remained stable, due to the bizarre dictatorial rule of Dr José Gaspar Rodríguez de Francia, who closed Paraguay off from the outside world until his death in 1840.

Spain

The loss of the colonies devastated Spain. Diplomatically, Spain was confirmed as a minor power, barely worthy of notice. Spanish ability to influence international affairs was distinctly limited. For most of the post-Napoleonic powers, about the only point of interest was maintaining a Bourbon family upon the Spanish throne. If there was a silver lining, it was the retention of Cuba, Puerto Rico, and the Philippines as colonial possessions. The Philippines only suffered one brief disturbance in 1823 that was easily put down. Cuba and Puerto Rico, heavily garrisoned in comparison with the other colonies and fearful of a Haiti-like uprising by the relatively large slave population, had remained steadfastly loyal throughout the conflict. Many ex-Royalists settled in Cuba and Puerto Rico, and in the 19th-century "Great Game" of European empire-building and colonial expansion, these territories at least put Spain at the table. However, while France had recovered sufficiently from

Napoleon's defeat to seize Algeria in 1830, Spain would not gain any new territories until 1859, when a series of conflicts began for possession of Morocco.

Financially, the loss of colonial trade eviscerated the Spanish economy, which had never recovered from the war with France. Spain fell into severe, persistent depression. Overall trade in 1827 was 75 percent less than in 1792, while exports were down 90 percent. The port city of Cádiz was particularly hard hit. As the traditional center of American trade, she had been the crown jewel of Spanish mercantile activity. With the end of the trade monopoly, much of which involved re-exporting foreign goods to America, the sizeable foreign population departed. Industry, especially shipbuilding, collapsed. Out of 300 shipbuilders before the wars, only 20 were left in 1824; 227 of 623 merchant companies went bankrupt. Similar disruptions were felt everywhere – textile production in Catalonia and Andalucia collapsed. Silk production in Seville fell by almost 85 percent, while cotton products almost disappeared altogether. Other staple products such as wine, olive oil, and brandy also suffered decline. Some newspapers and officials saw an opportunity to reinvent a Spain that had grown economically stagnant, reliant upon agriculture rather than industry and import/export duties rather than developing high-quality Spanish-made products. Unfortunately, the problems were too vast, and Spain settled into the secondary, if not tertiary, tier of European economies well into the 20th century.

Ferdinand VII was able to reassert and retain absolute monarchy but at a huge cost. Personally reviled, Ferdinand maintained power only by a combination of ruthless repression and the continued presence of French troops. A man not known for doing much of anything successfully, it is hardly surprising that his last major decision was a disaster. Having no male heir, succession became a crucial issue. In 1830 Ferdinand reinstituted a decree originally issued by his father, Charles IV, allowing a female

This 1848 photograph shows San Martín, long retired to France but still exhibiting a general's proud demeanor. (Museo Histórico Nacional, Argentina)

to become heir to the throne. That same year his wife gave birth to a daughter, whom they named Isabella. This had the effect of eliminating Ferdinand's brother, Carlos, from the line of succession. Oddly, Carlos was the favored candidate of the Absolutists who had maintained Ferdinand since 1814. When Ferdinand died on September 29, 1833, Isabella was named queen with her mother, Maria Christina, as regent. Carlos' supporters took arms. The dispute led to the Carlist Wars, a series of three debilitating civil wars that raged between 1834 and 1876, further crippling the nation.

Upon his resignation in 1822, San Martín remarked: "My youth was sacrificed in the service of Spain and my middle age in that of my country. I think I have a right to my old age" (Lynch 2009: 192). Unfortunately for most of San Martín's contemporaries, the war of independence did not mark the end of their struggles, only the beginning.

Bibliography

Archival and primary sources

Archivo General de Indias, Seville.

Anon., ed. (1965). *Las Fuerzas Armadas de Venezuela en el Siglo XIX*, vols I–IV. Caracas: Presidencia de la Republica.

Cajigal, Juan Manuel (1960). *Memorias del Mariscal de Campo Don Juan Manuel de Cajigal Sobre la Revolución de Venezuela*. Caracas: Ministerio de Justicia.

Chesterton, George Laval (1853). *Peace, War and Adventure: An Autobiographical Memoir*. 2 vols. London: Longman, Brown, Green & Longman's.

Cushing, Caleb (1833). "Reminiscences of Spain, the Country, It's People, History and Monuments," *The North American Review*, Vol. 37, No. 80: 84–117.

Hamilton, Colonel J.P. (1827). *Travels Through the Interior Provinces of Colombia*. 2 vols. London: John Murray.

Hidalgo y Costilla, Miguel (2007). "Manifiesto del Señor Hidalgo, contra el edicto del Tribunal de Fe," *Colleccion de Documentos Para La Historia de la Guerra de Independencia de Mexico*. Autonoma de Mexico: Universidad Nacional.

Luna, Felix, ed. (1954). "Memoria Militar del General Pezuela (1813–1815)," *Revista Histórica*, Vol. XXI: 164–273.

Miller, John (1829). *Memoirs of General Miller*. London: Longman, Rees, Orme, Brown & Greene.

O'Leary, Daniel Florencio (1883). *Memorias del general O'Leary*. 32 vols. Caracas: Imprenta de "El Monitor."

O'Leary, Daniel Florencio (1970). *Bolivar and the War of Independence*. Austin, TX: University of Texas Press.

Poinsett, J.R. (1825). *Notes on Mexico Made in the Autumn of 1822*. London: John Miller.

Urdaneta, Rafael (1972). *Archivo del general Rafael Urdaneta*, Vols I–III. Caracas: Republica de Venezuela, Ediciones de la Presidencia.

Secondary sources

Albi, Julio (1990). *Banderas olvidados: El ejército realista en América*. Madrid: Ediciones de Cultura Hispánica.

Appel, John Wilton (1994). *Francisco Jose de Caldas – A Scientist at Work in Nueva Granada*. Philadelphia, PA: The American Philosophical Society.

Bencomo Barrios, Héctor (2000). *Miranda y el arte militar*. Los Teques: Biblioteca de Autores y Temas Mirandinos.

Bethell, Leslie, ed. (1985). *The Cambridge History of Latin America*, Vols I–III. Cambridge: Cambridge University Press.

Blanchard, Peter (2008). *Under the Flags of Freedom: Slave Soldiers & the Wars of Independence in Spanish South America*. Pittsburgh, PA: University of Pittsburgh Press.

Blossom, Thomas (1967). *Nariño – Hero of Colombian Independence*. Tucson, AZ: University of Arizona Press.

Chambers, Sarah C. & John Charles Chasteen, eds (2010). *Latin American Independence: An Anthology of Sources*. Indianapolis, IN: Hackett Publishing Co.

Chasteen, John Charles (2008). *Americanos: Latin America's Struggle for Independence*. Oxford: Oxford University Press.

Costeloe, Michael P. (1986). *Response to Revolution: Imperial Spain and the Spanish American Revolutions, 1810–1840*. Cambridge: Cambridge University Press.

Delmar, Alexander (1875). "The Resources, Productions and Social Condition of Spain," *Proceedings of the American*

Philosophical Society Vol. 14, No. 94
(January–June 1875): 301–43.

Descola, Jean (1968). *Daily Life in Colonial
Peru 1710–1820*. London: George Allen &
Unwin Ltd.

Fehrenbach, Charles Wentz (1970). "The
Liberal Opposition to Ferdinand VII,
1814–1823," *The Hispanic American
Historical Review* Vol. 50, No. 1
(February 1970): 52–69.

Gomez, Ana Margarita (2007). "The Evolution
of Military Justice in Late Colonial
Guatemala, 1762–1821," *A Contracorriente*
Vol. 4, No. 3 (Winter 2007): 31–53.

Harvey, Robert (2000). *Liberators: Latin
America's Struggle for Independence*.
Woodstock: The Overlook Press.

Helg, Aline (2004). *Liberty & Equality
in Caribbean Colombia, 1770–1835*.
Chapel Hill, NC: University of North
Carolina Press.

Henderson, Timothy J. (2009). *The Mexican
Wars for Independence*. New York, NY:
Hill & Wang.

Kinsbruner, Jay (2000). *Independence in
Spanish America: Civil Wars, Revolutions
and Underdevelopment*. Albuquerque, NM:
University of New Mexico Press.

Lasso, Marixa (2006). "Race War and Nation
in Caribbean Gran Colombia, Cartegena,
1810–1832," *The American Historical
Review* Vol. 111, No. 2 (April 2006):
336–62.

Lea, Henry Charles (1899). "Hidalgo and
Morelos," *The American Historical Review*
Vol. 4, No. 4 (July 1899): 636–51.

Lecuna, Vicente (1950). *Crónica razonada
de las guerras de Bolívar*. New York, NY:
The Colonial Press Inc.

Lee, Sidney, ed. (1894). *Dictionary of National
Biography, Vol. XXXVII*. New York, NY:
Macmillan & Co.

Luqui-Lagleyze, Julio Mario (2005). *Por el rey,
la fe y la patria: El Ejército Realista del Perú
en la Independencia Sudamericana,
1810–1825*. Madrid: Ministerio de
Defensa.

Lynch, John (1986). *The Spanish American
Revolutions 1808–1826*. New York, NY:
W.W. Norton & Co., Inc.

Lynch, John (2007). *Simon Bolivar: A Life*.
New Haven, CT: Yale University Press.

Lynch, John (2009). *San Martin: Argentine
Soldier, American Hero*. New Haven,
CT: Yale University Press.

McFarlane, Anthony & Eduardo
Posada-Carbo, eds (1999). *Independence
and Revolution in Spanish America:
Perspectives and Problems*. London:
Institute of Latin American Studies.

Madariaga, Salvador (1952). *Bolivar*.
New York, NY: Schocken Books.

Means, Phillip Ainsworth (1918). "Race
and Society in the Andean Countries,"
The Hispanic American Historical Review
Vol. 1, No. 4 (November 1918): 415–25.

Means, Phillip Ainsworth (1919). "The
Rebellion of Tupac-Amaru II, 1780–1781,"
The Hispanic American Historical Review
Vol. 2, No. 1 (February 1919): 1–25.

Pérez Tenreiro, Tomás (1971). *Don Miguel de
la Torre y Pando: Relacion de Sus Campañas
en Costa Firme 1815–1822*. Valencia:
El Ejecutivo del Estado Carabobo.

Riaño, Camilo (1973). *El teniente general
don Antonio Nariño*. Bogotá: Imprenta
y Litografía de las Fuerzas Militares.

Ruiz Moreno, Isidoro J. (2005). *Campañas
militares argentinas: La política y la guerra*.
Buenos Aires: Emecé.

Semprún, José (1998). *Capitanes y Virreyes:
El Esfuerzo Bélico Realista en la Contienda
de Emancipación Hispanoamericana*.
Madrid: Ministerio de Defensa.

Semprún, José (2002). *La División Infernal –
Boves, vencedor de Bolívar*. Madrid:
Ediciones Falcata Ibérica.

Slatta, Richard W. & Janes Lucas De
Grummond (2003). *Simon Bolivar's Quest
for Glory*. College Station, TX: Texas A&M
University Press.

Williams, Mary Wihelmine (1920). "The
Ecclesiastical Policy of Francisco Morazon
and the Other Central American Liberals,"
The Hispanic Historical Review Vol. 3, No. 2
(May 1920): 119–43.

Index